TEAM SPORTS

for girls and women

TEAM SPORTS

for girls and women

CAROLE L. MUSHIER
STATE UNIVERSITY OF NEW YORK
CORTLAND

Photographs by William Clymer ● Illustrations by Jean Putnam

WM. C. BROWN COMPANY PUBLISHERS
Dubuque, Iowa

PHYSICAL EDUCATION

Consulting Editor
Aileene Lockhart
University of Southern California

HEALTH

Consulting Editor
Robert Kaplan
The Ohio State University

PARKS AND RECREATION

Consulting Editor
David Gray
California State College, Long Beach

Copyright © 1973 by Wm. C. Brown Company Publishers

Library of Congress Catalog Card Number: 72—81628

ISBN 0—697—07260—6

Printed in the United States of America

Contents

Contents

Illustrations

Preface

This book is designed to assist in the understanding, presentation, analysis, and teaching of team sports. The student preparing to become a teacher, the beginning teacher in a school situation, the experienced teacher desiring new or review information, the recreation leader and instructor in the community, club, or camp situation, and the performer who wishes to improve her performance will find value in the contents.

The book attempts to go beyond a simple analysis of techniques to a discussion of how each *logically* fits into the whole game, what problems may arise with individual performers, and practical ways to help others achieve skillful play.

It is recognized that each group of learners is different. Generalizations and specifics are cited, however, to assist the teacher in meeting these situations.

It is strongly recommended that current rule books accompany this text. The Division for Girls and Women's Sports of the American Association for Health, Physical Education, and Recreation publishes rule books that are appropriate for each sport. This text is not a condensed rule book. Specific rules are presented in italics, however, when they determine ways in which skills are performed or strategies developed. Rules do change from time to time, and it is the obligation of the teacher to be knowledgeable about the current rules.

Any new ideas or thoughts which are presented here are due, in great part, to many rewarding experiences with fine students and colleagues and as a result of the sharing of reactions, participation, and interest with them. To these persons deep appreciation is expressed.

C.L.M.

Cortland, New York

Acknowledgments

The author is indebted to many persons who have directly and indirectly made this book possible.

Specifically, appreciation is due Aileene Lockhart who suggested that the book be written and has continued to give support and valuable suggestions as consulting editor for Wm. C. Brown Company Publishers; Wayne E. Schotanus, editor for Wm. C. Brown Company, for his patience and assistance; William Clymer of the Learning Resource Center, SUNY at Cortland, for his excellent photographs; the students of SUNY at Cortland who served as subjects for the photographs; Jean Putnam, Central Washington State College, for the fine drawings; and Mrs. Eva Norton who typed the manuscript.

And, finally, gratitude is expressed to friends and colleagues who encouraged and reacted to the content of the book, particularly Dolores A. Bogard, SUNY at Cortland; Betty J. Hileman, Central Washington State College; and Katherine Ley, SUNY at Cortland.

Introduction

This chapter presents an overview of the book. It is important that chapters one and two be read before the sports chapters so that the reader can understand why the latter are organized as they are and can, as a result, gain the greatest benefit from them.

Chapter two deals with a discussion of selected principles of learning as well as with the basic organization for teaching, drill formations, and suggestions for evaluating progress. Some of these principles are well known—so well known that they are often forgotten. Although much research has accumulated in the area of learning, the application of this research is not always clear.

Eight team sports are included. Basketball, field hockey, lacrosse, softball, and volleyball appear in separate chapters, while soccer, speedball, and speed-a-way, because of their similarities, are combined in one chapter.

Each sports chapter includes a brief introduction to the sport, selection and care of equipment, basic field or court dimensions and markings, underlying skill requirements necessary for play, analysis of skills, progression and teaching suggestions, drills for skill development, basic unit plan, and selected bibliography.

The presentation of skills is divided into basic or beginning, intermediate, and advanced levels of play. The basic or beginning skills are those which are necessary to play a regulation game. The intermediate skills may or may not be more difficult than the basic skills but represent those skills that enhance play and are not absolutely required to play the beginning game. Selected advanced skills are presented for the skillful player and may or may not be taught in a basic instructional program. These are the skills of the competitive, highly skilled performer. This book is primarily directed toward the teacher in the instructional program rather than toward the coach of a competitive team, but it is hoped that it may also be an aid to the latter.

Skills are organized in a teaching progression rather than by types or classification. Modified games and a section on the first regulation game situation are then placed to coincide with the progression. In this manner, an attempt has been made to make each skill, group of skills, and the game meaningful to the learner and logical to the whole teaching outline.

Sections on progressions and teaching suggestions include common mistakes made by beginners on each skill. These point out the areas where emphasis is needed during the initial presentation and ongoing teaching process. When a "whole" skill is considered too large for a beginner to assimilate, suggestions are given for the accumulation of "parts" to eventually make the "whole." A discussion of "whole" and "part" learning appears in chapter two.

Official rules often determine how a specific skill may, or even must, be performed. In these cases, the specific rule is indicated by italics in the body of the analysis. This, along with discussion of the skill, presents some of the "whys" for performing skills in certain ways.

It should be stressed that most analyses of techniques in textbooks are of necessity generalizations. No two players will perform any one skill in an identical manner. Allowances must be made for individual differences in strength, flexibility, speed, and agility. For this reason, skill analyses cannot be considered absolute; nevertheless, physical laws and mechanical principles (e.g., gravity, centrifugal force, efficiency of movement, effectiveness of the skill, limitations of the rules, and progression to higher levels of skill) fortunately permit some generalizations.

Drills utilizing game situations are strongly recommended. No drill should encourage incorrect mechanics, hamper further development, or require responses to stimuli that are in opposition to those required in the game itself. Relays often encourage incorrect mechanics, as it is natural for participants to attempt to win the race. Practice of modified skills may result in habits that are difficult to break and thereby may hinder further skill development. Drills that require students to react to the ball in ways that are not typical of the game may cause confusion in the game when the same stimulus requires a different response (see discussion of transfer in chapter two). It is far easier to learn a technique correctly in the beginning than to learn an "easier" version that will eventually require the breaking down of a habit and the relearning of the correct skill.

Conditioning for play can occur through the use of gamelike drills and progression of skills, or it can consist of exercises and tasks that may be unrelated to actual skill development. With the emphasis on early game play, it is recommended that conditioning be a part of the skill learning situations. Each drill should be demanding, yet not exhausting, and should be conducted as soon as possible at the speed required by the game. Thus, drills and beginning game play itself can develop the conditioning necessary to proceed to higher levels of play.

Sample unit plans that are included in each sports chapter give an outline of the content that may be covered in each of eighteen lessons. They are meant to be used as guides and cannot account for every situation.

Principles of Learning Applied to the Teaching of Team Sports

Motor learning has received much attention in recent years, though it has been studied in various disciplines for many years. Only recently, however, has the general physical educator taken interest in serious study of the relationship of motor learning to physical education. Part of the problem has been semantic. The methods course, traditionally a part of most professional preparation programs, has been concerned with motor learning: how people learn and how this learning can be accomplished most efficiently and effectively. Methods and motor learning, however, are not synonymous. A suggested definition of motor learning is: that total process, comprised of physiological and psychological elements, which results in a relatively permanent change in observed or potential movement behavior as a result of practice. The study of motor learning is not concerned with the organization of the class situation as represented by such things as how to take roll or whether groups should be divided into squads, as a methods course might be. It is concerned with areas such as theories of learning, plateaus and learning curves, transfer of training, generality versus specificity, motivation, and other matters essential to the learning of skills.

It would be an impossible task to cover in one chapter all areas of motor learning and their application to the teaching of team sports. Therefore, the purpose of this chapter is to present *selected* areas and applications with the hope that they will spark the reader's interest and promote further reading and understanding.

The interrelationship of the many factors affecting learning is inescapable. While each factor is discussed here separately, it should be remembered that the human being is a *total* functioning organism, often greater than the sum of its parts.

LEARNING CURVES

The plotting of a learning curve is simply a graphic display of performance over a period of time. It is possible for different curves to result from the learning of the same skill when different variables are introduced, for example, whole versus part learning; massed versus distributed practice; age and skill of learner; and high motivation versus low motivation. The variables are unlimited; some are controllable, some are not. Ideally, the teacher attempts to effect the greatest amount of learning in the shortest amount of time.

3

Types of Learning Curves

No single curve of learning fits all situations and learners. Figures 2.1, 2.2, 2.3, and 2.4 represent the four most common forms of learning curves.

Types of Learning Curves

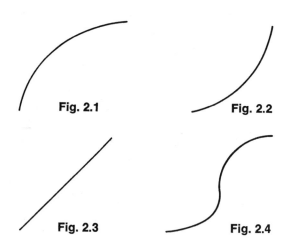

Fig. 2.1   Fig. 2.2

Fig. 2.3   Fig. 2.4

Figure 2.1 represents the "typical" or negatively accelerated curve. It shows an early rapid increase followed by a general tapering off. This curve is typical of a relatively simple task which permits a fast rate of skill development to relatively high levels, but improvement diminishes as the skill is mastered.

Figure 2.2 illustrates the positively accelerated curve typical of a relatively difficult task. Performance levels are low in the beginning, and rate of improvement is slow.

Figure 2.3 represents a linear curve typical of tasks requiring increasing strength in which learning appears to progress at a constant rate.

Figure 2.4 is an S-shaped curve which combines the qualities of the preceding three curves. Learning begins slowly as in the positively accelerated curve, becomes linear, and then shows a negative acceleration phase. This type of curve may appear in complex skill learning.

Obviously, no one learner will produce a smooth learning curve. Smooth curves are the result of averaging performance over a period of time. No two performers will progress at the same rate, although curves will be similar, but generalizations about the progress of a group of learners on specific skills are possible.

Plateaus

A plateau represents a stable performance level over a period of time after accelerated improvement in performance. A plateau can occur at any point in learning and may last differing amounts of time before there is further improvement. Although actual plateaus rarely appear, most performers have experienced the frustration of practice with little or no observable improvement.

There are a number of theories as to why a plateau may occur. Plateaus may represent the integrating of parts into wholes. It is possible that certain habits must precede the integration of patterns at higher levels and that plateaus, therefore, may represent a fixation at one level. Plateaus may represent a loss of motivation or interest; they may be the result of fatigue; they may represent bad habits, acquired during early learning, that hamper progress. One or all of the foregoing possibilities may explain the occurrence of a plateau.

Discussion

While it is not realistic to suggest that each individual's learning progress on each skill be plotted as a learning curve, an understanding of the learning curve and plateaus may enhance both the learner's and the teacher's understanding of the learning process.

For relatively simple skills, it is realistic to expect a fast rate of skill development. If it does not occur, the presentation of the skill and the learner's understanding of what is expected of her should be reviewed for flaws. It is unrealistic to expect "instant" success in complex motor tasks. The teacher must be careful in classifying the degree of difficulty of skills. To the accomplished performer, all skills may appear simple.

Plateaus in required instructional classes may be caused primarily by loss of motivation or interest or both. Many students may not "care" whether or not they improve, and as a result, progress is nil. Learning is an internal process; it cannot be forced on someone when she is resisting. In spite of the many discussions in the literature indicating plateaus, many motor learning theorists today believe that true plateaus do not exist, that learning continues although it may be difficult to measure or is not apparent to the teacher or learner.

TRANSFER

Transfer can be defined as the effect practice of one task has upon the learning or performance of another task. Some learning theorists do not believe transfer can occur, assuming that all learning is specific to the task. According to these theories, if transfer does take place at all, it is limited to small identical elements within the different tasks. Other theories, however, imply that transfer can occur on the basis of general instructions, common patterns, relationships, or configurations. The study of transfer has intrigued researchers for over seventy years. Most educational systems and theories of child development rely quite heavily on the concept of transfer.

Transfer can be positive, negative, or zero. Positive transfer occurs with the same response to different stimuli rather than with a different response to the same stimuli. The latter can produce negative transfer. The higher level of original learning achieved in the initial task, the greater the amount of possible transfer. Massed practice may produce negative transfer. Transfer occurs best from complex to simple tasks. The greatest possibility for positive transfer and the least possibility of negative transfer occur when the learner is aware of the transfer possibilities.

Discussion

The phrase "Teach for Transfer" has been used many times. Unfortunately, it has rarely been explained, and students are usually totally unaware of transfer possibilities. The teacher must understand transfer and the student must be aware of the possibility for transfer in order to take advantage of it. A serve in tennis may be like a serve in volleyball, but if the learner is not aware of the similarity, it will take her longer to recognize this fact. *But,* there are also subtle differences in the various overarm patterns of the volleyball serve, volleyball spike, lacrosse overarm throw, lacrosse overarm shot, softball overarm throw, and basketball overarm pass. These differences can cause negative transfer if the learner or teacher or both believe that the patterns are *identical.* The teacher must have more than a superficial knowledge of the skills involved.

MOTIVATION

Motivation is customarily defined as a general level of arousal in preparation for action. The motivated person is in a state of readiness or performance "set." Since what is learned is in response to the learner's goals and values, motivation is not an external or a superficial thing. The task to be learned, therefore, must have meaning for the learner. Some specific conditions have been suggested that affect the motivation to move:

1. Restriction from movement may act as a motive to move.
2. Fatigue can act as a negative motivator.
3. Reward and punishment can act as positive or negative motivations.
4. The learner's knowledge of results can affect motivation.
5. The level of aspiration of the learner affects motivation.
6. Success or failure can cause positive or negative motivation.
7. Motivation can be affected by competition, praise, participation, and cooperation.

The performance of a task depends primarily upon skill and motivation.

Discussion

Every education student has been told, at one time or another, that she must be able to "motivate" her students to learn. Too often, this is *all* that she is told. It is conceivable that each student in a class is motivated differently, and as a result, the teacher cannot be satisfied with an attempt to provide only one type of motivation, for example, using praise, and trusting that it will affect all learners equally.

Some degree of success or promise of success, or both, in the near future is important to most learners. It is suggested that early presentations include skills that can be learned fairly quickly by most students. The presentation of skills too complex can discourage the beginner. Realistic goals should be set by the teacher and the learner. The student must feel that she has "a chance" of reaching her goal and that the teacher is truly concerned with her attempts and progress. Most students respond to praise, and it is possible to find something to praise in even the most awkward attempts of a beginner. However, this can be overdone by reaching a point of insincerity, which can have the reverse effect on the student. There are a number of ways that the learner can evaluate progress and know the results of her efforts. Reinforcement of behavior can come from her own observations, comments from the teacher, and performance in task-oriented problems that indicate the level of performance.

The teacher cannot force motivation on students, nor can she act in ways that are unnatural for her. If a teacher is sincerely enthusiastic about teaching and students, conveying this enthusiasm to students may be the greatest motivation.

GENERALITY VERSUS SPECIFICITY OF PERFORMANCE

Such terms as *motor educability* and *general motor aptitude* are seldom seen in the current literature except in historical discussions. Most research points to the specificity of motor tasks. There are low correlations between abilities in various motor activities. The individual who is highly skilled in several activities probably possesses a number of specific underlying qualities such as strength, speed, and reaction time, rather than a general motor ability. These abilities, coupled with extensive practice and a high level of motivation and interest, can account for the "natural athlete" in a far more realistic fashion than does a theory of some type of innate general ability.

Some students appear to possess a "game sense" that far exceeds their skill ability and experience in the particular sport. Again, this student, rather than being a "natural athlete," has usually had a great deal of experience and success in other related areas and possesses the underlying knowledge of offense, defense, use of space, and awareness of others that can be applied in a new situation.

WHOLE AND PART LEARNING

The discussion of "whole" versus "part" learning is concerned, to a great degree, with a discussion of Gestalt or Field theories of learning versus Stimulus-Response or Bond theories of learning. Most educators adopt an eclectic point of view, using one or the other or both as the situation demands. The greatest danger is that the educator may not know why she does this and may not even be aware that it is occurring.

Despite much research in the area, there is disagreement on: what is a "whole" and what is a "part"; when a whole can be divided into parts; and how this division should be made.

The differentiation of whole and part depends on the task, the age and experience of the learner, and the knowledge and experience of the teacher. Often, the extent to which the learner is able to concentrate on a task, or memory span, is used as a determiner rather than a logical breakdown of a whole. Is a two-step landing a part of the lay-up shot or is it a skill, a whole, unto itself? The answer is that it is both, depending on the situation. Can a beginner handle the "whole" pattern of a lay-up shot without first learning some of its parts? This will vary with the learner and the teacher. Unfortunately, the answers are not clear-cut and well defined. The learning situation demands that teacher and student must carefully examine the situation and each task and then apply logical tactics to best achieve skillful performance. As a guide, the following is offered as an operational definition: A *whole* is a sequence of movements, that may be discrete or continuous, which can stand as a purposeful act unto itself. A *part* is a recognizable segment of a whole which may or may not stand as a purposeful act unto itself when removed from the context of the whole.

It is generally agreed that a discrete movement whole can be segmented into its parts without hindering the final learning of the whole. Team sports contain few discrete movements. The more typical movement pattern is a continuous action in which each part is a cue to the next. Timing, flow, and kinesthetic perception are often interrupted when a continuous whole is broken into parts for practice. The highly skilled performer can be the exception. In order to polish a skill, the highly skilled performer can often benefit from the practice of one segment of a skill without destroying the pattern. In this case, the timing is already developed, and part practice of even a continuous movement pattern can be beneficial.

HABITUAL AND PERCEPTUAL SKILLS

It has been suggested that all movement skills can be placed on a continuum from habitual to perceptual. Habitual skills are those skills that require a mechanical style which can be reproduced consistently with the conditions and environment relatively stable. Perceptual skills, while patterns of movement, require that the performer select the correct movement at the correct time in response to a changing environment. No skill is completely habitual or perceptual, but all skills do fall on a continuum between the two extremes. Team sports, particularly those with direct interaction of teams, such as basketball, field hockey, soccer, and lacrosse, are high on the perceptual side. Volleyball and softball, as sports with less direct interaction, fall more toward the habitual. The pitch in softball and the serve and set in volleyball depend a great deal on mechanical style that can be replicated in a fairly consistent environment. The tackle, pass, or shot in field hockey, lacrosse, soccer, and basketball must be performed with opponents and teammates moving and never in the same relationship and, therefore, are more perceptual skills.

The point in classifying skills is to suggest that different types of skills may be learned best in different ways. In primarily perceptual activities, the reactions or responses cannot be set, as they depend upon the particular situation. It seems unlikely that a performer could practice *every* situation in which the skill might be used. The stimulus-response type of practice might be of value in very early learning, but the effective use of the skill would require a generalized understanding of relationships and environment so that the correct movement could occur at the correct time. This suggests a holistic approach to the teaching of these skills. Skills that are ranked more toward the habitual end of the continuum

may benefit more from repeated practice of the isolated skills in a stimulus-response form to achieve a mechanical precision.

It is necessary to repeat that very few, if any, skills are purely habitual or perceptual. However, a skill or sport in which the performer must respond to an action of someone else tends to emphasize the perceptual. Situations that are initiated by the performer tend to be habitual.

The highly skilled performer, in attempting to correct minor flaws in technique, may benefit from repetitive practice in a static environment of a perceptual skill. The beginner, however, may find learning and application difficult under the same conditions.

SPEED AND ACCURACY

When a skill requires a certain degree of speed and accuracy to be effective, there are various means to achieve the combination. The typical methods used include emphasis on accuracy with speed developed after accuracy is achieved, emphasis on speed with accuracy developed after speed is achieved, and emphasis on both speed and accuracy. Emphasis on accuracy without speed often requires that the movement itself and the associated timing be altered in order to develop the required speed. In actuality, this requires the learning of two skills rather than one. The same problem exists when skills are practiced in slow motion. Slow, carefully executed movements require different neuromuscular patterns than those movements performed at game speed. It is highly impractical, therefore, to practice skills in slow motion or with a disregard for the speed element. Emphasis on speed with no concern for accuracy can have mixed results. In some activities this practice can be dangerous to the performer or to others in the area. Complete lack of control can also create the same type of situation as slow motion. It would seem, therefore, that a skill requiring both speed and accuracy should be practiced under conditions that emphasize both requirements. Basically, this means that all skill practices should be under gamelike conditions as soon and as often as possible. If a dribble is to cover space and move the ball quickly, then it should be practiced under these conditions. There is a question as to how much speed is enough and how much is too much. This varies with each skill, but the following can serve as a guideline: Speed of practice should approximate the normal requirements of the game as closely as possible yet permit a reasonable amount of control for the safety and satisfaction of the performer.

PRACTICE SCHEDULING

Much research has been conducted concerning the benefits of massed versus distributed practice, but the results are often contradictory and misleading. There are a number of questions that have not been answered: What is massed practice and what is distributed practice? Is it possible to generalize from practice on simple fine motor tasks to complex gross motor skills? Is the effectiveness of the type of practice specific to the task? Until the answers to these questions are available, it is difficult to accept any definitive statements. With these limitations, the following are offered for possible application to the learning of complex sports skills: Massed practice may be more effective when the learner is highly motivated; Distributed or spaced practice may be best when the task is difficult, fatiguing, or the learner is not highly motivated.

EXPLORATORY MOVEMENT AND PROBLEM-SOLVING

Exploratory movement and problem-solving have received much attention as *methods* of presenting and teaching. It must be emphasized that these methods are not casual approaches to teaching but require *much* planning and consideration on the part of the teacher. These methods can effectively involve the learner in the learning process by having her develop her own learning process with guidance. The procedure is different from the widely used explanation—demonstration—drill method. Rather than the very lengthy explanation and demonstration that are typical of beginning teachers, the learner is given some basic parameters within which the problem (skill) must be solved. For example, in teaching the dribble in field hockey, the following parameters could be given to beginners: The stick must be held in two hands; Only the flat side of the stick can be used; See how fast you can get from point *A* to point *B*, hitting the ball on the ground. Permit the participants to experiment with this, answering any questions that individuals might ask. Then add further parameters, such as working with a partner, and what adjustments must be made to prevent her from getting the ball. After experimenting with this, the participants should be ready to discuss what has happened. Suggested questions for discussion are: Which hand positions permitted you to hit the ball most easily and with control?; What was the fastest way of getting from point *A* to point *B*?; What type of dribble kept your opponent from getting the ball? At this point, suggestions for effective and efficient ways of dribbling under different circumstances will be more meaningful for the learners. The learners can participate in the discussion and ask relevant questions because they have had some experience with the task. Rules that affect the dribble now will place further parameters on performance of the skill. Further practice would include these parameters.

There are endless ways to utilize this method. There are no set patterns and no incorrect performances when students meet the parameters as set down. This method does require planning, creativity, and imagination on the part of the teacher.

CLASS ORGANIZATION

Good planning and well-considered class organization are imperative if the learning situation is to be effective. It is true that there are conditions over which the teacher may not be able to exert complete control. All teachers are aware of the difficulties of very large classes, very small classes, mixed age groups, mixed ability groups, and inadequate facilities and equipment. Whether or not any or all of these situations exist, the learning situation must be made as effective and attractive as is possible under the existing circumstances, and efforts should be made to improve undesirable and unstimulating conditions.

Class Size

In team sports classes, the ideal class size is two teams plus a number equal to the average number of students not in attendance each day. In the team sports requiring small numbers, such as basketball and volleyball, four or even six teams plus extras can be handled if facilities and equipment are adequate. On the other hand, it is very difficult for one teacher to give adequate individual attention or even appropriate supervision to more than one field of players in field hockey, lacrosse, soccer, softball, speedball, or speed-a-way.

Class Grouping

There are both advantages and disadvantages to homogeneous or heterogeneous grouping by age or skill. The most typical arrangement in school situations is homogeneous grouping by age or grade. Such an arrangement provides some similarity of social experience and class instructional background of students but does not allow for differences in learning or out-of-class experiences. In most cases, homogeneous grouping by age or grade produces a heterogeneous grouping of skill levels. This type of grouping can cause the more highly skilled to become bored or disinterested and the lesser skilled to "give up." However, it is possible to challenge the higher skilled while they in turn provide a pattern and motivation for the lesser skilled. There is something to be said about the old maxim heard so frequently in tennis but applicable to all areas, "Always find someone better than yourself to play with if you wish to improve." This is not as possible in team sports when groups are organized according to skill level, but one must be careful not to abuse the more skillful individual who appears good-natured about playing with less skilled individuals.

In general, a combination of heterogeneous and homogeneous grouping may be the best solution. In many school and club situations, large groups of students are divided among several teachers. Then there is the opportunity of grouping by skill level for initial instruction, followed by more heterogeneous grouping for further development. The opportunities are unlimited, even with one group and one instructor. Different groups may practice together at different times, thereby permitting many different combinations.

EVALUATION OF PROGRESS

Learning can only be inferred from performance. While learning is considered relatively stable, performance can be erratic. Performance tests of sports skills have been employed for many years. A number of these tests have been devised by individual teachers and may or may not have acceptable validity or reliability or both. For true evaluation of progress, these types of tests may have limited value. As motivational and feedback devices for the learner, however, they may be invaluable.

It is recommended that both student and teacher evaluation of progress be a continuous, ongoing process. Evaluation should not be a procedure, out of context from the usual instruction and practice, that is only employed at the end of a unit. Evaluation or knowledge of results of performance should provide feedback that is essential to the learner. Some primary means of achieving feedback can occur through simple observation of results—"Did the ball go into the basket?"; from external comments by the teacher—"Try placing your hand here"; from comments by other students—"You missed!"; by watching video tapes of performance; and by performance on standardized tests.

When performance on skills tests is delayed until the last day or week of a unit, the results do not have much effect on the progress of the learner and simply become a device that somehow determines a grade. How unfortunate that skills tests can become very external and meaningless. Skills tests, such as those published by the AAHPER Sports Skills Project Committee, can be one means used for continuous, ongoing feedback for the learner and for teacher-student evaluation of progress. The AAHPER tests are designed to be used as practice devices while, at the same time, providing feedback and evaluation from objective measures and norms.

DRILL FORMATIONS

Basic drill formations are mentioned in the sports chapters. These include the following:

1. *Informal grouping in twos.* Players are instructed to spread out within a given area in twos. Spacing can be formalized, if there is inadequate space or if safety is a matter of concern, by placing the players in two lines facing each other, each opposite another player.
2. *Informal grouping of more than two.* Groups are instructed to spread out within a given area. In cases where the safety of players is a concern due to the nature of the activity (e.g., batted balls), the groups should all hit in the same direction or spread sufficiently to prevent interaction of the groups.
3. *Relay formation.* Lines of players, one player behind another in each line, facing the same direction, one person from each line performs at the same time.
4. *Shuttle formation.* Two lines of players face each other over a specified distance, one player behind another in each line.

5. *Circle formation.* Players are in small circle groups or the entire group is in one large circle of a specified size.

Other drill formations are described when they appear in the body of each chapter.

It is possible to become so concerned with formations that little practice occurs. There are many times when an informal breakdown into small groups, twos, or ones for a few minutes may be far more efficient than an elaborate organization of players into specific lines or areas. Certainly the nature and purpose of the skill and its practice will determine the way in which the players are organized. It is often necessary, for the safety of the participants or the nature and purpose of the practice, or both, to have all players performing the same thing, at the same time, in the same direction, within a certain designated area. It is beneficial, however, to vary the situation and not regiment or overorganize a practice that does not warrant it. Learning is an internalized affair and overorganization can dampen natural enthusiasm.

Basketball

Basketball is a popular team sport for girls and women in the United States. The game was developed in 1891 by James Naismith and colleagues to provide a recreational activity for YMCA male trainees. Women teachers observed the game, and a small group organized the first women's basketball team. The first scheduled competition was held in March 1892.

Women's basketball has been plagued with many different sets of rules from its inception until the present day. The first set of rules was published in 1895, and since that time, there have been a multitude of interpretations, misinterpretations, and sets of rules operating concurrently in different sections of the country.

The two primary rule-making bodies in women's basketball have been the Division for Girls and Women's Sports (DGWS) of the American Association for Health, Physical Education, and Recreation (AAHPER) and the Amateur Athletic Union (AAU). Although these two groups differed concerning the rules and standards for play, in 1964 compromises on both sides resulted in identical rules. Since 1968, a joint DGWS-AAU basketball rules committee has represented the interests of most girls and women engaged in basketball. How-

ever, other sets of rules that govern girls' and women's play in basketball still exist. Some are sponsored by state high school associations, individual states, counties, and even city, school, and recreational systems. In the opinion of many experts, the multiple sets of rules have held back the development of competition in girls' and women's basketball, particularly at the international level. This chapter refers only to the DGWS-AAU rules.

Basketball for girls and women has traveled a very arduous course from the three-court, nine-player teams to the present five-player teams.

EQUIPMENT

Balls

A round ball weighing 20 to 22 ounces, measuring 29½ to 30¼ inches in circumference, and bouncing 49 to 54 inches when dropped from a height of 6 feet is official for the game. The ball may be covered with leather, rubber, or synthetic material. Balls should not be stored in excessively hot or dry areas. They may be cleaned with a soft damp cloth or, in the case of leather, with saddle soap.

13

Uniforms

Teams should wear uniforms of contrasting colors with a number on the front and back of the uniform in a solid color contrasting to that of the uniform. The number on the back should be at least six inches high, the number on the front at least four inches high. Pinnies may be worn to distinguish teams, and for official play they should have official-size numbers front and back.

Uniforms should permit freedom of movement. Some one-piece gym wear does not permit a great amount of stretching or bending. The typical basketball uniform is shorts and shirt.

Each player should have good quality footwear. Most popular are the various leather shoes designed specifically for court play.

Backboards, Baskets, Court, and Markings

The white or transparent backboards, usually rectangular in shape, measure four feet high by six feet wide and are suspended four feet inside the court from the end line. The lower edge of the backboard is nine feet from the floor. The backboard, whether rectangular or fan-shaped, is constructed from glass, wood, or other suitable material. The baskets are attached to the backboard with the ring ten feet from the floor. The rings should be bright orange and the nets white cord.

The court and markings are shown in figure 3.2. The official court is seventy-four to ninety-four feet long and forty-two to fifty feet wide. The overhead clearance should be at least twenty-two feet. All lines should be well defined and two inches wide. If possible, there should be an unobstructed area of ten feet outside the boundary lines of the court. The playing surface should be smooth and free from any foreign material (e.g., oil, water, and chalk).

UNDERLYING SKILL REQUIREMENTS

Basketball requires shooting, catching, and throwing a rather large ball, and the ability

Fig. 3.1. Rectangular backboard and basket.

Fig. 3.2. Court and marking

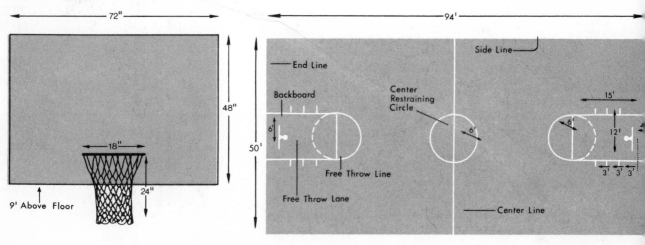

to move quickly in any direction, including jumping upward. Players are required to move up and down the length of the court, with or without short rests, for four eight-minute quarters. Endurance and conditioning are necessary prerequisites, as is a certain degree of strength to handle the ball. Quick starts, agility, short bursts of speed, explosive strength for jumping, and perception of spaces and players moving in a relatively small area are among the necessary skills of a successful basketball player.

SKILLS

This section contains beginning, intermediate, and advanced skills. The skills are organized in a logical teaching progression rather than by function. The beginning skills are those skills necessary to play a basic official game. The intermediate and advanced skills are an important part of the total game and allow the player to cope with a greater variety of situations. The beginning skills remain basic to play at any level.

Each skill is described in terms of its use and then is analyzed and followed by suggested progressions for learning and teaching. Appropriate drills follow each skill. Modified and first game situations are included at logical points in the presentation of skills. Emphasis is on gamelike situations early in the experience of the learner.

Beginning Skills

The skills absolutely necessary to play a beginning official game are catching, basic pass, short and moderate distance shots, and basic footwork for control. Although guarding is imperative for the game, the game can be played before actual instruction in this skill.

CATCHING

Catching the ball is essential for team play in basketball. The easiest catch is a ball that arrives about chest level. The catcher attempts to get behind and in line with the ball. As the ball approaches, the catcher extends her arms toward the ball, with the elbows in an easy, not fully extended, position. The fingers are relaxed and spread. The ball is caught with the fingers and thumb on either side of the ball in position

Fig. 3.3. Catch

for a pass. The palm rarely touches the basketball. The speed of the ball determines the amount of "give" necessary in the direction of the flight of the ball. A lightly tossed ball requires very little, if any, give of the arms toward the body. If the approaching ball is below chest level, the fingers should point downward for the catch.

PROGRESSION AND TEACHING SUGGESTIONS

The most common errors in catching a basketball are:

1. Holding the arms and fingers stiffly extended in preparation for the catch.
2. Shying away, ducking, or closing the eyes prior to the catch.
3. Pointing the fingers directly at the oncoming ball.

Some girls and women are afraid of the impact of the basketball, particularly if their first experiences have been with hard-thrown balls that they have caught incorrectly. For those who are afraid and for beginners, it is suggested that they be given the opportunity to catch lightly tossed balls to get the "feel" of catching. Catching the ball is absolutely essential for all players.

DRILLS

Drills for catching a basketball are best incorporated with drills for passing. However, beginners may form small circles, with a player in the center, and practice catching a ball lightly tossed underhand by the player in the center.

CHEST PASS

The chest pass is considered the basic pass in basketball. The player is in position for this pass after a two-hand catch, and the position for the chest pass is the ready position from which the player can pass, shoot, or dribble. The chest pass is accurate over moderate distances. Players will soon learn their own limitations in terms of distance over which this pass can be used.

The ball is held in front of the body at chest level with hands *slightly* behind the ball. The fingers are spread comfortably with the thumbs pointed at an upward angle toward each other. The ball is held by the fingers and thumb. The ball does *not* rest in the palms. The pass is initiated by a dropping of both wrists as the ball is brought slightly toward the body. The arms begin to extend forward in the direction of the pass, accompanied by an uncocking and subsequent flicking of the wrists inward. Both arms exert equal force in a parallel action. On the follow-through, both arms extend in the direction of the pass, fingers extended and thumbs down. The ball leaves the fingertips last, providing final accuracy. On the pass, beginners should be encouraged to step forward with either foot, providing greater impetus for the pass. As players advance in skill, a quick, short pass can be executed without a shift of weight.

PROGRESSION AND TEACHING SUGGESTIONS

The most common errors in performing the chest pass are:

1. Gripping behind the ball and attempting to push it forward.
2. Cocking the wrists upward instead of down in initiating the pass.
3. A lack of wrist action, resulting in a weak pass.
4. Pushing the ball with one arm more than the other, resulting in an inaccurate pass.
5. Holding the upper arms parallel to the ground with elbows out, resulting in a lack of power.

The mechanics of the chest pass are most difficult to describe. For many years, a circular motion was advocated for initiating the pass. Since a circular movement beginning down and toward the body could be

Fig. 3.4. Chest pass

accomplished without changing the position of the wrists, the procedure hampered rather than helped the correct technique for the chest pass. Circular movements of all sizes emerged, with greater concentration on this motion than on the pass itself. It is suggested that the drop of the wrists be emphasized without mention of a circular motion. The chest pass is a direct pass. Over short distances there should be little arc in the flight of the ball.

DRILLS

1. In twos, pass back and forth over ten to fifteen feet.
2. In circles, with one player in the center, the pass goes from center to a player

and back to center, progressing around the circle. After each round, a new player goes into the center.

3. In circles, players pass as quickly as possible to any other player in the circle.
4. Two lines of four to six players are formed, each player in one line facing a player in the opposite line approximately ten to fifteen feet apart. Starting with the ball at one end, it is passed back and forth up and down the lines.

As the techniques of the skill are learned, drills number 2 and 4 can be utilized as re-lays, provided the skill itself is not permitted to break down.

TWO-STEP STOP

When a player has possession of the ball, there are limitations by the rules on her subsequent movement. *A player may take two steps after receiving the ball in the air, on the run, or on the completion of a dribble.** A violation of this rule is called travel-

* Italics indicate rules that determine the performance of skills.

Fig. 3.5. Two-step stop

ing. Therefore, it is very important that the player become aware of the rules limitations early in her experience in basketball. Since beginners seem to have a great deal of difficulty with traveling, it is recommended that a two-step stop be emphasized from the beginning.

A two-step stop is best taught when a player is receiving a pass on the run, and later when completing a dribble. As the ball approaches in the air, the receiver running toward the ball hops on one foot, timing the hop so as to catch the ball when both feet are off the ground. The ball is caught, and the player returns to the ground on the hopping foot for her first step. The second step is taken with the opposite foot into a forward stride position. The hop transforms some of the forward momentum to upward momentum and acts as a brake. The hop also makes the player aware that only two more steps will be legal.

PROGRESSION AND TEACHING SUGGESTIONS

The most typical errors in the two-step stop are:

1. Hopping too soon and catching the ball after the first step has been taken.
2. Hopping too late, after the ball has already been caught.
3. Becoming confused as to which foot will be the hopping foot.
4. Leaping rather than hopping. The hop requires that the player land on the take-off foot. In the leap, the player lands on the opposite foot.
5. Taking more than two steps following the catch.

Awareness of the two-step stop is crucial to the game. The two-step stop as presented in the previous section is *one* method of achieving this awareness. It is *not* the only method of stopping. A player may simply take two strides to stop. However, traveling is very common for beginners, and a stylized technique can aid in the control of their feet. Players tend to prefer one foot, but from the beginning, they should be taught to hop on *either* foot rather than adjusting their stride to hop on the preferred foot. The hop is similar to the half gallop that younger children use when pretending to be a horse. The pass to the player should be an arcing soft pass so that the receiver has the feeling of hopping *up* to receive the pass. This will help in the timing of the hop. If players are taking more than two steps after the hop, they might count out loud "one—two" as their feet hit the floor. It may also help if the second step is emphasized with a slightly harder step to remind the beginner that it is her last step. For receiving and passing while on the run, the player catches in the air, takes two steps, and releases the pass just after the second step. This can be practiced in a shuttle line formation that requires each player to move forward for the pass, receive, and pass to the next approaching player.

DRILLS

The following drills represent a progression for the two-step stop. It may be advisable to present the underhand pass before the two-step stop, as the chest pass will be difficult for players to catch in the beginning stages of the two-step stop.

1. In small circles or one large circle, players execute a continuous half gallop, hopping on the same foot. Repeat, hopping on the opposite foot.

2. As a continuation of drill number 1, players are instructed to mimetically catch a high, soft pass each time they hop up in the half gallop. Repeat, hopping on the opposite foot.
3. From a well-spaced line, facing across the floor, players run forward and execute a two-step stop, mimetically catching a ball on command. Emphasize the use of either foot.
4. In short lines with the first player approximately ten to fifteen feet in front facing the line, each player moves forward to catch a high, soft pass from the first player. For the first trials, each player comes to a full legal stop, counting out loud or emphasizing the second step or both if necessary, passes back to the first player and goes to the end of her line. As players become proficient, the return pass should be executed directly following the second step, negating the need to come to a complete stop. The passing position should be rotated periodically.
5. In shuttle formation, two lines of players facing each other, players execute a continuous catch—two-step stop—pass, each player going to the end of the opposite line. The lines will tend to get too close as the drill progresses and will have to adjust back. Observation of others may be valuable at this point. Every other shuttle group sits and observes the next group performing. Comments and discussion should follow each group.

UNDERHAND PASS

The underhand or "flip" pass is only useful over very short distances. It may be easily blocked or intercepted if used over longer distances, since the ball moves slowly and tends to arch. It is most effective when a player is moving toward the passer and is three to eight feet away.

From the basic ready position of holding the ball with two hands about chest level, the player prepares to pass from directly in front of her body or brings the ball across to one side of her body, usually the side closest to the receiver. The ball is turned so that one hand is under the ball, the other on top. The ball is thrown with a flipping motion, much like a softball pitch, with the upper hand guiding the ball. Players should be able to pass the ball from either side of their body, depending on the position of the receiver. The ball may also be passed with two hands on either side of the ball from in front or from the side of the body. This pass is often referred to as a two-hand underhand pass.

PROGRESSION AND TEACHING SUGGESTIONS

The most common errors in the underhand pass are:

1. Using too much wrist action, flipping the ball too high.
2. Taking too large a backswing in preparation for the pass.
3. Attempting to pass underhand over too great a distance.

While the underhand pass can be effective over short distances, it is not as fast or direct as other passes over moderate to long distances. It is often used by a post player as a handoff to a cutting player. Because the pass does tend to arch, it is a useful pass for early practice of a two-step stop.

In shuttle formation, players execute continuous underhand passes.

At intermediate and advanced levels, the underhand pass can be incorporated with high post drills.

LAY-UP SHOT

The lay-up shot is the basic close shot of the game, executed from a pass or a dribble.

The technique of the lay-up shot is just what its name implies—the object is to lay the ball up against the backboard so that it will rebound into the basket. The two-step stop technique can easily be modified to provide the footwork for the lay-up shot.

The player, moving toward the basket at approximately a forty-five-degree angle, hops on the same foot as the shooting hand to receive the pass or to catch the ball after her last dribble. To protect the shot, the right hand is the shooting hand when ap-

Fig. 3.6. Lay-up shot

proaching the right side of the basket; the left hand is the shooting hand when approaching the left side of the basket. The player lands on her hopping foot for the first step and on the opposite foot, striding toward the basket, for her second step. Instead of stopping on the second step, the forward momentum is transferred upward in a jump from this foot. The point of take-off with the second step will vary with the amount of forward momentum, but the jump should position the player in the air close to the side of the basket. As the two steps are taken, the ball is raised until it is well over the head on the jump. Both hands are on the ball, the shooting hand behind and under the ball until the point of release. The ball is released at the height of the jump, with the shooting arm fully extended to lay the ball against the backboard. If there is no spin on the ball and the player is approaching at a forty-five-degree angle, the ball should hit the backboard slightly above and to the right of the basket. The object of the lay-up shot is for the player to be as high as possible on the release in order to reduce the distance over which the ball must travel and therefore reduce the possibility of error. As the player varies the angle of her approach, she must change the point of impact on the backboard accordingly. A player approaching directly toward the center of the basket should attempt to lay the ball just over the front rim of the basket rather than aim for the backboard.

PROGRESSION AND TEACHING SUGGESTIONS

The most common errors in the lay-up shot are:

1. Shooting too far away from the basket.

2. Jumping too late and being too far under the basket for the shot.
3. Not transferring forward momentum to upward momentum thereby not achieving the highest possible jump or causing the ball to hit the backboard too hard.
4. Shooting with the same hand from both sides of the basket.
5. Traveling while attempting the lay-up shot.

The progression from the two-step stop to the lay-up shot is a natural one. It is suggested that the hop—step—step—jump be taught in the beginning. Later, players may modify to a two-stride takeoff without the hop. The use of the left *and* right hands, with the appropriate footwork, should be stressed from the beginning.

DRILLS

1. In twos or short lines, facing a wall or open space, one player passes the ball to the approaching player who goes through the footwork and release of the lay-up without actually shooting at the basket. Practice should include the use of both hands as shooting hands.
2. Practice as in number 1 except that lines are formed at a forty-five-degree angle to the basket. One player can pass the ball for each line, with other players rotating through the position of passer. This can be modified by having each player, after she shoots, be responsible for retrieving the ball and giving the next pass.
3. Two lines are formed, each at a forty-five-degree angle to the basket on opposite sides, one line acting as retrievers and passers, the other line as shooters. Each person goes to the end of the opposite line. Beginning concepts of re-

bounding can begin at this point with the object being that the ball should never hit the ground during the drill.

4. Various tasks can be attempted by individuals or groups—ten consecutive successful lay-ups from a pass on the left, right, and center; ten successful lay-ups from a dribble; or counting how many attempts a player requires to reach ten successful lay-ups.

ONE- AND TWO-HAND SET SHOTS

The term *set shot* implies that a shot is taken for the basket from a stationary position. Set shots can be taken from moderate to long distances away from the basket and are used as free throws after a foul. Although beginners will need only one type of shot that can be used when too far away for a lay-up in very beginning play, two types are presented here. Some beginners may not be able to control a one-hand set shot, while others may prefer it. Therefore, a basic one-hand set shot or a basic two-hand chest shot or both may be introduced at this point.

The one-hand set shot can be described as a one-hand push shot. The ball is held about head height, slightly toward the side of the shooting hand. The shooting hand is behind and below the ball, with the ball resting on comfortably spread fingers pointed upward, and the wrist is hyperextended. The nonshooting hand supports the ball from underneath. The shooter is in a forward stride position, with the foot on the shooting side forward. As the ball is brought to head height, the knees bend. As the knees extend, the ball is pushed up and forward by the shooting arm, finishing with a flexion of the wrist. The fingertips provide control and direction as the ball leaves the hand. The follow-through is in the direction

Fig. 3.7. One-hand set shot

of the basket. On longer shots, the player may leave the floor to provide greater power. Since the basket must be entered from the top, the flight of the ball should be a high arch just over the front rim of the basket. Flat shots or shots that travel in a rather direct line toward the basket are low percentage shots.

The two-hand chest set shot is similar to the chest pass. The major difference is the flight of the ball. The shot should be directed upward in an arc, with the arms following through in the direction of the shot.

In all shots, other than a lay-up shot, the highest point of the arc of the ball should be just over half the distance between the player and the basket. The point of aim is just over the closest part of the rim, not the backboard.

PROGRESSION AND TEACHING SUGGESTIONS

The most common errors in the one- and two-hand set shots are:

1. Throwing the ball in the general direction of the basket rather than shooting in a controlled manner .
2. Attempting too long a shot.
3. Shooting with a flat arc.
4. Causing the highest point of the arc of the ball to be too close to the basket, resulting in a high hit on the backboard.

Although shooting requires the strength necessary to put the ball into the air over a distance, successful shooting also requires a fine touch and precision given by the wrist and fingers. Requiring players to shoot from long distances often destroys precision. Each player should start within a comfortable range and progress to greater distances at her own rate. Some players will find difficulty with the one-hand shot, and others with the two-hand shot. The one-hand shot has some greater possibilities for transfer to other types of shots.

Slight backspin on the ball helps to prevent drifting and causes the ball to rebound toward the basket if it hits the backboard.

DRILLS

1. In twos or small groups, players shoot high, arching shots to each other or against a wall.
2. In small groups, players form a semicircle around the basket, inside the free throw line, with one or two players to retrieve and return the shots. Emphasis is on technique, not distance, and players rotate around the semicircle. Each player determines her own distances.
3. It is possible to play a number of relay, novelty, and modified games at this point. While these may be fun and beneficial, it is recommended that players experience a game close to the regulation game as soon as possible.

FIRST GAME SITUATIONS

It is possible to begin regulation-type play when the players can catch, pass, control their movements, and shoot. While some might feel that dribbling is essential to the game, beginners tend to overuse this skill and destroy the passing element of the game. As a result, they do not develop the teamwork necessary for successful play. Dribbling is not required by the rules; therefore, the beginning game is developed best without dribbling.

Beginning play will suffer from the lack of coordinated offense and defense. In the interest of permitting the players to play the game as soon as possible, the following can be used as guidelines:

1. Match players from opposite teams, instructing them that they are responsible for "being with" their opponents when the opposing team has the ball. Their job is to try to prevent the player from re-

ceiving the ball and, if she does have the ball, to prevent her from passing or shooting, without coming in contact with her. Although this will be far from adequate as a defense, it will point out to the players the need for instruction in defensive techniques and systems.

2. The team with the ball is instructed to move the ball, by passing, as quickly as possible toward their basket, always attempting to evade their opponents. They will need to be reminded that the object of the game is to put the ball into the basket.

3. The playing situation can be controlled by having two teams play on one half of the court. This will also permit more players to play at one time. For a half-court game, the opposing team receives the ball for a "free" pass at the center line after a basket.

Basic rules for out-of-bounds and traveling are used. Free throws for fouls can be introduced at this time, including the lineup of teams. Other rules and basic strategy are best introduced as the situation occurs. A discussion with the players following the first game situation will provide the opportunity to stress basic elements and to answer questions, and may prove enlightening to the players and the instructor.

Intermediate Skills

Intermediate skills are a vital part of the game but are not required by the rules to play the game. They will permit the player to cope with a greater variety of situations that occur in the game.

DRIBBLE

The dribble is the primary means by which the individual player can move with the ball on the court. It must be stressed that beginners tend to overuse this skill, which can

Fig. 3.8. Dribble

make the game very individualistic rather than a team game.

Players should be able to dribble with either hand and should practice this from the beginning. The dribble is the repeated bouncing of the ball. *The dribbler may initiate the dribble with one or both hands, but the dribble ends when the dribbler again touches the ball with both hands or causes it to come to rest in one hand.* The dribble is executed with the fleshy part of the fingers. The palm does not touch the ball. The ball is not slapped or beat, but rather, it is stroked with the pads of the fingers in a controlled manner. The fingers and wrist are loose, yet controlled. The height of the bounce varies with the speed of the dribble and the proximity of opponents. Generally, the ball is not bounced higher than the waist. When protecting the ball from a nearby opponent, the dribble is low and close to the body on the side away from the opponent.

PROGRESSION AND TEACHING SUGGESTIONS

The most common errors in dribbling are:

1. Slapping at the ball rather than stroking it.
2. Bouncing the ball too high.
3. Dribbling in place rather than using the dribble to cover space.
4. Watching the ball rather than watching the other players on the court.
5. Using one hand to the exclusion of the other hand.

Although most players enjoy the prospect of dribbling, the skill must be practiced over a period of time before it enhances rather than hinders play. Most beginners fix their attention and eyes solely on the ball. They must be encouraged, from the beginning, to look up between dribbles, eventually being able to dribble while focusing attention on the developing play. Backspin on the ball decreases the distance that must be covered in order to retrieve it; forward spin increases the distance.

DRILLS

1. In small groups, players dribble the ball in place, using left and right hands.
2. In short lines, players dribble the ball across the court, using left and right hands and looking up between dribbles.
3. In short lines, obstacles (other players, chairs, etc.) are placed in the path of the dribbler. The dribbler dribbles on the side away from the obstacle, alternating sides.

DEFENSIVE TECHNIQUES

While systems of defense are described in the section on defensive strategy, there are certain individual defensive techniques basic to all systems.

The basic defensive stance is one which permits the player to move in any direction depending upon the movement of her opponent and the ball. The defensive player is in a comfortable stride, with knees slightly bent, leaning forward from the waist. Her arms are extended in an attempt to be as large an obstacle as possible. *It is illegal to impede the progress of a player by holding both arms extended horizontally.* Therefore, the most effective position of the arms is with one high above the head, the other about waist height. The high arm blocks possible shots or passes, and the low arm protects against low passes or a dribble.

The player must be able to move forward, backward, and to either side with equal facility. Most players will need to practice moving backward in a balanced position. Weight must be kept forward, otherwise the player will lose her balance backward. Players should never cross-step when moving to the side, as this commits movement in that direction, and it is difficult to recover quickly if the opponent shifts direction. Defensive players use a shuffle step in which the lead leg moves in the intended direction, and the trailing leg closes to the lead leg without crossing in front or back of the lead leg.

While these movement fundamentals are essential for defensive play, offensive play also utilizes these movements.

PROGRESSION AND TEACHING SUGGESTIONS

The most common errors in individual defensive techniques are:

1. Allowing the center of gravity to shift back while running backwards, resulting in a loss of balance.
2. Crossing the legs when running sidewards.
3. Failing to keep the arms extended.
4. Guarding too close to a player who may still legally dribble the ball.
5. Flailing the arms in the air rather than following the ball with one hand.

Individual defensive techniques are basic to any system of defense. Players must actually practice running and moving in all directions with arms extended. It is not uncommon to hear "Arms up!" as a reminder to defensive players even in advanced competition. It is a natural tendency to keep the arms low for balance.

DRILLS

1. Players spread over the floor and move left, right, front, and back, on command.
2. In short lines, relays are used over short distances, with players running backwards and running sidewards.
3. In partners, one player dribbles the ball; the other player attempts to stay between the dribbler and the other side of the court. This can become a one-on-one drill with the offensive player attempting to make a basket.

PIVOTS AND FEINTS

Pivots and feints are protective and deceptive techniques for the offensive player. A pivot is a turn made with one foot in contact with the floor to protect the ball from opponents or to be in a better position to pass or shoot. *A player may use either foot as a pivot foot after catching the ball while standing still or after coming to a stop in the first step. A player may pivot only on the rear foot after a two-step stop.* A rear or back pivot indicates that the movement of the free leg is to the rear. A front pivot is one in which the free leg moves forward. In preparation for a pivot, the player, in the ready position, shifts her weight over the nonpivoting foot. This leg is used to push off in the desired direction, with the ball of the pivoting foot remaining in contact with the floor.

A feint is a deceptive movement in one direction to draw the defensive player to that direction. As the defensive player shifts, the offensive player is free to move in another direction. The most common feint is with the ball. The offensive player moves the ball as if she were going to pass or dribble in one direction, hoping the defensive player will commit herself to that side. The feint can be left, right, high, or low, and may consist of a series of movements. The offensive player may combine the feint with the ball with a slight shift of weight or lean in the direction of the feint. Beginning defensive players usually key on the ball; therefore a feint with the ball may be most effective. More advanced players may key on the hips, making a ball feint less effective. Defensive players who watch the eyes of opponents can be easily faked by a look in one direction and a pass or move in another. The offensive player must determine the most effective means to feint against different opponents. There is danger in beginning play that a player can become so intrigued with feinting that too much time is taken before a pass, dribble, or shot. A feint is done with intent and design and should not become an aimless moving of the ball in all possible directions.

DRILLS

1. Players spread over the floor and pivot on command.
2. Use one-on-one play, emphasizing feinting and pivoting. This can also be utilized in two-on-two play.
3. Set plays involving feint and pivot, for example, player dribbles, stops, feints one direction, pivots to opposite direction, and shoots.

BOUNCE PASS

The bounce pass is a one- or two-hand pass directed toward the floor, causing the ball to bounce between the passer and the receiver. Because of the trajectory of the ball, the bounce pass is slower than a direct pass

and is, therefore, more easily intercepted. It is an effective pass when an opponent is between the passer and the receiver but should not be used if a direct pass is possible.

For the two-hand bounce pass, the player is positioned as for the chest pass. The pass is executed in the same manner as the chest pass, except that the ball is directed to hit the floor approximately two-thirds of the distance between the passer and the receiver. The ball is released low, directed toward the floor, with a step in the direction of the pass.

The one-hand bounce pass is executed with a sidearm delivery. From a ready position, the ball is taken to one side of the body at waist height. A step is usually taken to the side of the ball, and the ball is brought forward with a sidearm delivery. The throwing hand is behind the ball, and the wrist and fingers give final impetus to the ball.

PROGRESSION AND TEACHING SUGGESTIONS

The most common errors in the bounce pass are:

1. Pushing the ball rather than passing.
2. Throwing the ball to the ground rather than executing a pass that travels out and low.
3. Causing the ball to hit the floor too soon or too late in relation to the position of the receiver.

The bounce pass is a skill that can easily be overused. Once the bounce pass has been introduced, it is not uncommon for beginners to use it every time they pass the ball. Since it is a slow pass and easily intercepted, it should be reserved for the situation in which a direct pass is not possible. Because of its name, *bounce* pass, beginners may attempt to initiate the pass from a high position with hands on either side of the ball. This causes a relatively high bounce with little impetus in a forward direction. Although the ball does hit the floor in the bounce pass, it does so in a skidding motion with forward momentum.

DRILLS

Beginning drills for the one- and two-hand bounce pass may be the same as for previous passes. It is important, however, to practice the pass in the situation in which it is most effective.

1. In small circles, with one player in the middle, players around the circle attempt to pass the ball past the player in the middle to another player on the outside.
2. In threes or small groups, one player attempts to pass the ball to another player, with an opponent positioned between the passer and the receiver.

JUMP BALL

Although most players have been taught to jump from a stationary position, they should have the opportunity to practice the jump ball situation in basketball. The jumper positions with either shoulder

Right shoulder toward ball

Player on left began with opposite shoulder toward ball

Fig. 3.9. Jump ball

toward the ball. Players vary in their preference as to which shoulder is used. If the shoulder on the same side as the tapping hand is toward the ball, the player swings her arms upward as she jumps straight up and taps the ball at the height of her jump. If the opposite shoulder is toward the ball, the player turns in the air as she jumps straight up to a position facing the ball as she taps it. The most difficult part in the jump ball is timing the jump so that the tap occurs at the height of the jump with a fully extended arm. The hand and wrist direct the ball in the desired direction.

PROGRESSION AND TEACHING SUGGESTIONS

The most common errors on the jump ball are:

1. Jumping forward toward the ball rather than straight upward.
2. Mistiming the jump with the toss.
3. Batting at the ball indiscriminately rather than directing the ball in a specific direction.

Without specific instruction, beginners will tend to flail away at the ball on a jump ball, hoping just to hit it somewhere. They must practice with a controlled jump and specific objective to overcome this tendency. For practice in jump balls, all players can also be instructed in how to toss the ball for jump balls. The ball may be tossed with the tossing hand under the ball, the other hand on top for control, or with hands on the sides of the ball.

DRILLS

In threes or small groups, one player tosses the ball for two jumpers. Players should

experiment with different shoulders facing the ball. On the tap, players should attempt to send the ball to a particular place or player. Later, specific plays can be developed from the jump ball.

REBOUNDING

Once the ball has been released on a shot for the basket, both teams should attempt to receive the rebound should the shot be unsuccessful. Rebounding is primarily dependent upon positioning. The defensive

Fig. 3.10. Rebounding. White team on defense; dark team on offense.

team is most frequently in a better position to rebound, and therefore, defensive rebounds usually outnumber offensive rebounds. The two ideal positions for rebounding are just on either side of the basket, a few feet away from the backboard at a forty-five-degree angle. The angle and the type of shot will determine the most likely type of rebound. Rebounders should time their jump to catch the ball at the height of their jump with extended arms.

PROGRESSION AND TEACHING SUGGESTIONS

The most common errors in rebounding are:

1. Failing to react to the shot by positioning for the rebound.
2. Tapping or hitting at the ball rather than attempting to catch the ball.

Rebounding is often neglected in skill development. It cannot be assumed that players will automatically know how and when to rebound. Since correct positioning is the key to rebounding, this should be stressed. Defensive rebounders should position in such a way as to block out potential offensive rebounders, yet not so far away from the basket to permit a rebounder to be in front in good position to shoot.

DRILLS

While practice in rebounding can occur through play in the game, some specific practices can be used. Practice can occur from two-on-two through five-on-five play. To set up for the rebound, players face the player with the ball as in regular play. The ball is then tossed or shot at the basket, and players position for the rebound. The toss or shot should occur from varying angles.

OVERHEAD PASS

The overhead pass is a quick pass that can be thrown over the head of an opponent. It is particularly effective for tall players. With two hands, the ball is held above and slightly in front of the head. The hands are on each side, slightly behind and under the ball. From this position the wrists cock backward and the elbows flex slightly in preparation for the pass. The wrists uncock and the arms extend forward, propelling the ball in a direct pass. A step may be taken with either foot as the ball is released.

Beginners will tend to drop the ball behind their head in preparation for the pass. This slows down the execution of the pass and leaves the ball open to a player behind the passer. Rather than attempt to gain momentum from taking the arms back, beginners should place emphasis on the wrist action.

Practice in the overhead pass can utilize drills presented for previous passes.

OVERHEAD SET SHOT

The overhead set shot is similar to the overhead pass. The ball is held in the same manner, and the execution is the same except that the ball is directed in an arc toward the basket. Although the overhead set shot may be used by all players, it is most effective as a quick, moderate to short shot by taller players.

SHOULDER PASS

The shoulder pass resembles an overhand softball throw and is used over long distances. Since most strategy emphasizes short passes, the shoulder pass may have limited value. However, there are times in the game when a fast-breaking player may be free and well ahead of her opponents. At this point a long pass may be necessary. The ball is held over the shoulder on the throwing arm side of the body. The throwing hand is behind the ball with the wrist cocked back. The ball is released with an overarm throwing action as in the softball throw. Final impetus and direction are given with the wrist and fingers.

Selected Advanced Skills

The following skills may or may not be included in a typical instructional program. Since many girls and women are exposed to basketball instruction at early ages, it is quite possible that they will be ready for the challenge of more advanced skills in instructional and, certainly, in competitive programs.

JUMP PASS AND SHOT

The jump pass and shot utilize a one- or two-hand pass or shot combined with a jump. The object is to gain as much height as possible and release the ball at the height of the jump. The pass may utilize the two-hand overhead or one-hand pass. The jump shot may utilize a two-hand overhead set shot or a one-hand set shot. As the player jumps, the ball is brought up to the position for the pass or shot. At the height of the

Fig. 3.11. Jump shot

jump, just before the player begins to descend, the ball is released. The pass is direct, and the shot is arced toward the basket.

PROGRESSION AND TEACHING SUGGESTIONS

The most common errors in the jump pass and shot are:

1. Releasing the ball before the height of the jump.
2. Releasing the ball after beginning to descend to the floor.
3. Jumping forward rather than directly upward.

Players must be aware of the point in their jump when they are "hanging" in the air—neither going up nor coming down. It is recommended that players jump without a ball until they can "feel" this point. Next, they should attempt to release at the "hanging" point, mimetically—without a ball. The first attempts with a ball should be over short distances and may be directed at a wall or partner. Most girls and women do not have the power necessary to use a jump shot beyond the radius of the free throw line. Shooting practice should begin rather close to the basket.

HOOK SHOT

The hook shot is all but impossible to guard, yet very few girls and women have mas-

Fig 3.12 Hook shot

tered the shot. With the emphasis on post play and the adaptation of strategy of the men's five-player game, the hook shot will occupy greater prominence in the women's game.

The hook shot is a moderate to short shot and is effective when the shooter is closely guarded with her back to the basket. The shot is initiated with a step away or diagonally away from the basket with the foot opposite the shooting arm. As the step is taken, the shooter watches the basket over her shoulder and moves the ball to the shooting side of her body away from the basket. Both hands are on the ball for control, with the shooting hand under the ball. As the weight is taken on the striding foot, the shooting arm moves in a circular movement up from chest height to a position over and slightly behind the head. The ball is released as the player elevates the weight-bearing foot and is controlled by the fingertips and wrists.

Although the hooking movement can be compared with a slinging-type movement, the shooter does not "sling" the ball toward the basket. Rather, the hook shot is a soft shot, controlled by the fingertips.

Mastery of the hook shot can only occur after a great amount of practice. Players must realize the distance limitations of the shot, as it is rarely effective from long distances. Many teachers and coaches have discouraged the use of the hook shot because they believe it has a low percentage of success. This is true of any shot when players have not mastered the techniques.

VOLLEY PASS

The volley pass is a means of receiving the ball, controlling it momentarily, and sending it on to another player. It is effective only as a short-distance pass when the situation demands an immediate pass. To execute a volley pass, the player catches the ball in the usual manner, but the ball comes to rest only momentarily in the hands before it is redirected as a pass. The fingertips do not volley the ball as in a legal hit in volleyball. The volley pass is likened to an illegal hit in volleyball, with the ball coming to rest in the hands.

TIP-IN

The tip-in is a means of returning the ball toward the basket as a shot from a rebound without returning to the floor between the rebound and the subsequent shot. The player times her jump for the rebound to receive the ball just before the peak of her jump. The ball is controlled as in the volley pass—the ball coming to rest momentarily in the hands—and is directed back toward the basket just after the player has reached the peak of her jump. The timing of the jump is critical for the tip-in. Players who have mastered the jump shot can progress to the tip-in. A suggested progression is as follows:

1. In lines, jump shot against a wall, each player catching the rebound of the player in front of her and executing a jump shot.

2. In twos, first player executes a jump shot against the wall; the second player jumps to receive the ball and, while still in the air, directs the ball back to the wall. This can progress to lines of players attempting continuous tip-ins against the wall.

3. In twos or lines, one player throws the ball at the backboard; the next player attempts a tip-in.

STRATEGY

The team with the ball is on offense; the team without the ball is on defense, regardless of the position of the ball or players on the court. Basketball involves the direct interaction of players and teams. The game consists of four eight-minute quarters. Each field goal counts two points; each free throw counts one point. Each team attempts to score as many points as possible and to prevent the opposing team from scoring. It is toward these ends that all basketball strategy is aimed.

Basic strategy is basic to *all* levels of play. Basic strategies for offense and defense are presented in this section.

Offensive Strategy

The game begins with a center jump. At this point, theoretically, neither team is on offense or defense since neither team has possession of the ball. Since field goals can only be scored when a team has the ball, possession is the first maxim of the game. Once a team has the ball, their objective is to move the ball by passing and dribbling to a position from which a shot may be taken for a field goal.

One of the first considerations on offense is whether to use a series of set plays or a free-lance system. It is recommended that basic concepts be developed utilizing a free-lance system for beginning play. The offensive system should be as simple as possible. Set plays demand specific responses from players at specific times. If a team is operating on set plays and the play breaks down, they will find it difficult to continue the offense. A free-lance offense can utilize certain basic maneuvers such as screen, pick, fast break, and post players. Later, set plays

can also utilize these basic offensive maneuvers.

A *screen* is the setting of a stationary block on a defensive player, screening her out of the play so that an offensive player with the ball can shoot or drive for the basket.

Fig. 3.13. Screen for shot

A *pick*, sometimes called a screen and roll, or pick and roll, is a type of screen that allows the offensive player with the ball to move past a defensive player. It is usually employed for a drive toward the basket for a shot but can be used anywhere on the court to free a player. Rather than setting a screen directly between the player with the

Fig. 3.14. Setting the pick

cessful fast break, there should be no more than two defensive players between the three breaking players and the basket. The center player takes the ball down the center to the free throw line. If there is a great distance to cover, she can pass to one of the players on either side and then receive the pass back. If a defensive player does not move to guard the center player, she should shoot from the free throw line, and the other two players should attempt the rebound. If the center player does draw a

Fig. 3.15. Fast break

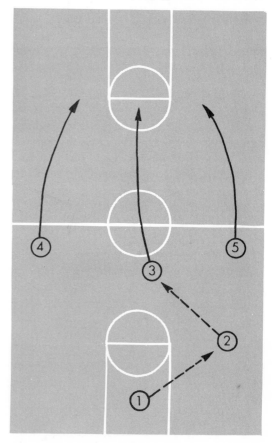

ball and the basket, the pick cuts off the path of the defensive player in the direction the offensive player is moving.

A *fast break* is a maneuver used to move the ball quickly down the court so as to have three offensive players against two defensive players. There are times when the ratio of offense to defense may vary, but the intention of the fast break is to have more offensive than defensive players. The fast break begins with a defensive rebound or interception. The ball is moved quickly to the side by a pass to another player or by the rebounder dribbling to the side. The pass is faster than the dribble. As soon as the rebounder gains possession of the ball, three players break for the center line. The pass should go to the player in the center breaking position. At this point, on a suc-

guard, one of the players on the side will be free for an easy shot.

The fast break can be a potent offensive maneuver. There are a number of modifications that can be made as players advance in skill. However, the basic concepts and formations of the fast break should be included at the intermediate level.

Post play refers to the positioning of players in or near the key when their team is on offense. Post players, or pivot players, permit a great number of options for the offense. The *high post* player is positioned at the free throw line, usually outside the key. In utilizing the high post, the object is to get the ball to the high post player. The high post player can shoot, drive to the basket on either side, pass to a cutting player, or pass the ball out. Each time the post player receives the ball, she can exercise one of these options. She can execute a screen or a pick for another offensive player most effectively. The *low post* player moves in and out of the key near the basket. A low post player in combination with a high post player is called a *double post*. The low post is often free for a pass and short shot when the guards are drawn toward the high post player.

The system of defense employed by the opposing team determines the type of offensive play that will be most effective. Against a player-to-player defense, the offense should utilize the screen, pick, and post play. Players must be able to move quickly and handle the ball skillfully to elude the ever-present opponent. The offense must play to the major weakness of the player-to-player defense, namely, the shift that must occur once a player breaks free of her opponent. This requires a passing and cutting game, with offensive players moving rather than being able to maintain relatively stationary positions.

Against a zone defense, the offensive players without the ball will not be closely guarded and therefore will have more freedom to move and receive passes. Although screens, picks, and posts can be used against a zone defense, one of the primary objectives should be to move the ball from one area of the court to another, causing the zone to shift rapidly. Since the offensive team can pass the ball more rapidly than the defensive team can shift, gaps will result in the defense. It is then that the offense capitalizes on these gaps with a cutting player. If a zone is tight toward the basket, the offense should attempt to open it up with moderate to long shots. If the zone is loose and away from the basket, the offense should send players cutting through for short shots. More than one offensive player in one zone is called overloading and can make defensive coverage difficult.

The five players on offense generally fall into the pattern of two forwards, a center, and two guards. The forwards' basic position is toward the corners of the court. They should be able to shoot set shots from the side of the basket as well as cut and drive toward the basket for short shots. The forwards are also responsible for offensive rebounds. The position of the center will depend on the type of offense. If she is a low post, she is positioned to one side of the key, close to the basket. She then moves through the key trying to get free for a pass. The two guards are primarily responsible for bringing the ball down court, and their basic position on offense is toward center court. Guards must be quick, good dribblers and able to take moderate to long set shots. One guard usually coordinates the offense.

GENERAL OFFENSIVE STRATEGY

1. A pass is faster than a dribble. Players should pass whenever possible.
2. Players should give "lead" passes to moving teammates.
3. All offensive players should watch the player with the ball while cutting.
4. Each shot should be a high percentage shot, but players should not lose sight of the objective of scoring baskets.

Defensive Strategy

Defense begins as soon as the ball is lost. Each player must be conditioned to change quickly from offense to defense. Defense demands teamwork, whether player-to-player or zone. Player-to-player is very demanding of each individual player. Zone defense, while more complex in concept and demanding in terms of all five players working as a unit, is somewhat less physically demanding of each individual player.

Player-to-player defense requires that each defensive player be matched with an opponent. The defensive players nearest the ball guard their opponents closely, while those away from the ball sag toward the basket in a position to pick up a free offensive player. Because each defensive player is basically responsible for one specific opponent, the player-to-player defense is the easiest for beginners to understand. *However,* unless all defensive players are quick and agile, a free offensive player can easily result in havoc in a beginning defense. If a defensive player loses her opponent, she should immediately drop back toward the key. The free player must be picked up by another guard who switches from her player to the free player. The "lost" defensive player now picks up the remaining free player. A screen or pick may cut off a defensive player, in which case the closest defensive player switches with the cut-off player to pick up her opponent. The defensive player guarding the player with the ball has the "right of way" and is allowed to move in front of other defensive players to maintain the best position.

Since beginning players can be quickly organized into a player-to-player defense, this system is often used when players first get into the game. A zone defense should be employed as soon as possible since it permits players of varying abilities to play more equally in the usual instructional class situation.

Zone defense requires a coordinated effort of all five defensive players at all times. A zone defense concentrates on the position of the ball. The player with the ball is actively guarded by the defensive player in that area, while the other defensive players position to cover spaces and intercept passes. The 2–1–2 defense positions two

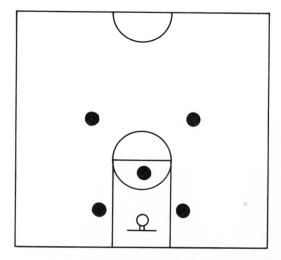

Fig. 3.16. Basic 2-1-2 defense

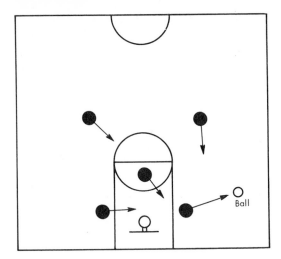

Fig. 3.17. Shift of 2-1-2 defense

GENERAL DEFENSIVE STRATEGY

1. Whatever system is employed, each player must understand her particular role.
2. If a player has not dribbled, she cannot be guarded as closely as is possible after she has dribbled.
3. The defense should force the opponents to pass and should attempt to intercept the passes.
4. The primary objective of the defense is to regain possession of the ball.

BASIC UNIT PLAN FOR BEGINNERS

While each teaching situation is unique, the following eighteen lessons represent a guide for instruction. It is assumed that some type of warm-up will precede each lesson. It is suggested that these warm-ups be as closely related to the game as possible. Review of previously presented skills should occur, based on student performance. Practice stations may be set up in different areas, permitting small groups to work on different skills. These practice stations can include tasks of a skill test nature. Although time is allotted for officiating, rules, and strategy, much of the basic coverage of these areas should occur as situations develop in play and as a part of skill presentations. Lessons should not be just endless practice of skills, but should allow for play whenever possible.

players beyond the free throw line, one player behind the free throw line in the center of the key, and two players back near the basket in rebounding position. Each player guards the player with the ball when in her area. When not actively guarding, the defensive players position to protect lanes to the basket and intercept passes. For example, figure 3.17 shows the movements of the defense from the basic position to one covering when the forward on the right side of the basket has the ball.

Other defenses include 1–2–2 and 1–3–1 zone defenses and a combination defense. Combination defenses utilize both player-to-player and zone defenses. One example is four players in a box zone defense with the fifth player opposing the strongest or key opponent player-to-player.

It is unlikely that many different systems of defense can be covered in the instructional class situation. It is recommended that a basic 2–1–2 zone defense or player-to-player defense, or both, be used in the class situation.

Lesson 1	Catching, chest pass, two-step stop
Lesson 2	Two-step stop, underhand pass, lay-up shot
Lesson 3	Lay-up shot, one- and two-hand set shots
Lesson 4	First game situation

SELECTED BIBLIOGRAPHY

DGWS. *Basketball Guide.* Washington, D.C.: American Association for Health, Physical Education, and Recreation. Published yearly.

MILLER, KENNETH D., and HORKY, RITA JEAN. *Modern Basketball for Women.* Columbus, O.: Charles E. Merrill Publishing Co., 1970.

NEAL, PATSY. *Basketball Techniques for Women.* New York: The Ronald Press Co., 1966.

SCHAAFSMA, FRANCES. *Basketball for Women.* 2nd ed. Dubuque, Ia.: Wm. C. Brown Co. Publishers, 1971.

WILKES, GLENN. *Basketball for Men.* 2nd ed. Dubuque, Ia.: Wm. C. Brown Co. Publishers, 1972.

WOODEN, JOHN R. *Practical Modern Basketball.* New York: The Ronald Press Co., 1966.

Field Hockey

Field hockey for girls and women is a popular team sport usually played in the fall of the year. Since its introduction in the United States by Constance Applebee in 1901, the game has spread from the East to all parts of the country. The number of school, college, and association players increases each year.

The United States Field Hockey Association (USFHA) was formed in 1922 and remains to this day the only national organization directly responsible for the rules and development of the game. The official rules are published every two years in the *Field Hockey–Lacrosse Guide* by a joint committee of the USFHA and the DGWS. In 1967, the USFHA adopted the rules of the International Federation of Women's Field Hockey Association (IFWHA). The same rules are used throughout the world by over thirty nations.

Women's field hockey and lacrosse are unique in that they are played solely within educational institutions at the junior and senior high school age levels. There are no clubs conducted by other groups at these levels. After graduation from high school, or its equivalent, a player may play for a college team or join a local association team directly related to the USFHA. Over one-half, approximately 1,000, schools and colleges conducting field hockey programs are allied with the USFHA. There are more than fifty local adult associations all over the country. National tournaments are conducted by the USFHA each year for college and association players who qualify. The first and reserve teams in the United States are selected at the tournament. These teams represent this country in international conferences, on tours, and in the United States opposing other national teams.

Field hockey in this country is played primarily by girls and women, although there are several men's field hockey clubs. Women have been responsible for the development, organization, teaching, and coaching of the game since its introduction in 1901.

EQUIPMENT

Balls

Official field hockey balls are covered with white leather. There are other types of balls available for practice, since leather balls tend to absorb moisture and must be painted to maintain their whiteness. Plastic-covered white balls are most popular for practice, as they require very little care and

41

Fig. 4.1. Equipment for field hockey

need only to be wiped with a damp cloth to remain white. In addition, they do not absorb moisture and may be a bit livelier than leather-covered balls. Composition balls are also available for practice but must be painted and do not last as long as those that are plastic-covered. Pudding balls are available for indoor practice.

Sticks

Field hockey sticks are usually made of ash or mulberry. There are no left-handed hockey sticks; all players must play with a stick that has a flat side on its left-hand side only. The length of a hockey stick varies according to the distance from a player's hand to the ground and her typical posture while playing the ball. It does not follow, therefore, that the taller the player, the longer the stick. Typical sticks are thirty-five to thirty-seven inches long and weigh eighteen to nineteen ounces. Shorter, lighter sticks can be purchased for elementary and junior high school players. The Indian-style, short-toed stick is preferred by most players today.

Hockey sticks should be stored in a cool, dry area. They should be hung or stood upright separately. Piling sticks in a box or similar container over a period of time may cause warping and in everyday use will cause the grips to wear out prematurely. Rubber grips will deteriorate over a period of time and can be replaced when necessary. Varnished sticks need only to be wiped dry. Unvarnished sticks should be waxed periodically to prevent the absorption of moisture. Any splinters or fraying should be sanded smooth. A stick that is cracked at the toe or in the shaft should not be used.

Shin Guards

Shin guards should be available for all players. Particularly in beginning play, they reduce bruises to the shin and instep and diminish the fear of injury. Good quality shin guards are relatively firm with leather or self-adhering straps. Buckles should be fastened on the outside of each leg. Shin guards that can be inserted under knee socks are also available.

Shin guards should be kept in pairs, buckled together and lying flat. They can be cleaned with a brush, and straps and buckles should be kept in good repair.

Shoes

Since field hockey is played on a grass surface, a good quality cleated shoe is recommended. There are several types available, including the typical black canvas shoe with molded rubber cleats, and the leather shoe with plastic, rubber, or leather cleats. Beginners should be encouraged to use cleated shoes, as they reduce the possibility of slipping and resultant injury. Recognizing that cleated shoes may not be a practical investment for beginners, many beginning players wear tennis shoes.

Goalkeeper's Equipment

Protective leg guards are available in various sizes for the goalkeeper. Care should be taken that the goalkeeper wears leg guards that cover her thighs. Protective covering for the feet may consist of goalkeeper's boots, a hard leather half boot, or padded canvas kickers. Leg guards and kickers should be kept clean and may be polished white so that the goalkeeper stands out as a target for shots at goal.

Uniforms

Any sport outfit that permits freedom of movement is appropriate for field hockey. Competitive teams find the kilt and blouse most popular. Since field hockey may be played in cool or cold weather, warm-up pants and jackets are essential under these conditions.

Pinnies with position letters on front and back may be used to identify players but are not required.

Field and Markings

A field hockey field is a level, grassy area one hundred yards long and sixty yards

Fig. 4.2. Field and markings

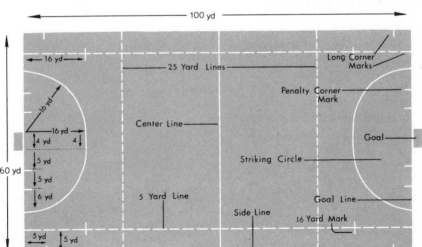

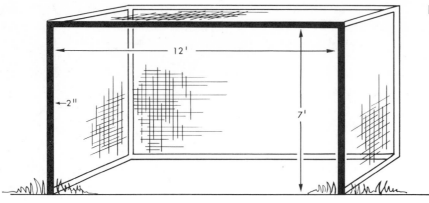

Fig. 4.3. Goal cage

wide. Markings three inches wide include sideline, goal lines, center line, dotted twenty-five-yard lines, dotted five-yard lines parallel to sidelines, and sixteen-yard striking circles in front of each goal. Other shorter lines indicate the position of the ball for corner hits, penalty corner hits, and defense hits. Four-foot-high flag posts are placed on all four corners and on the center line outside the field.

Goals

The field hockey goal is four yards wide and seven feet high. The posts and crossbar should be flat and measure two inches facing the field of play. Nets are usually attached to form a rectangular box, but the side facing the field remains open.

UNDERLYING SKILL REQUIREMENTS

Field hockey is a running game. While the skillful use of the stick is essential for highly skilled play, the prime prerequisites are speed, agility, and endurance. The of-

ficial game consists of thirty-five-minute halves without time-outs or regular substitution. Therefore, all players must be able to perform at game speed for more than thirty-five minutes. This can only be accomplished through conditioning for the game. A certain amount of strength is necessary to perform a hard drive and tackle. This strength is relative, however, and certain positions are more demanding than others. Players on both teams interact on the field; therefore, each player must be able to move within large and small areas and perceive spaces and other players as they move.

SKILLS

This section includes beginning, intermediate, and selected advanced skills. The beginning skills are those necessary to play a basic official game. The intermediate skills allow the players to cope with a greater variety of situations, and the advanced skills are presented for the player who has mastered the intermediate skills. The skills are presented in a teaching progression rather than in a grouping together of skills with common functions.

Each technique is described in terms of its use in the game, analyzed and discussed, then appropriate drills are given for practice. Common errors made by beginners are presented and discussed so that they can be anticipated and corrected early in the learning process. Emphasis is placed on gamelike situations as early as possible in the teaching progression.

Beginning Skills

The skills necessary to play a basic official game are grip and carry of the stick, dribble, fielding, and passing. Although dodging and tackling will become necessary, they are not required by the rules. Shooting for goal is accurate passing, and such techniques as roll-ins and free hits can be accomplished before actual instruction.

Fig. 4.4. Grip and carry

GRIP AND CARRY

The hockey stick is held in two hands and carried as close to the ground as comfortable. Players must be able to run at top speed, yet be ready to play the ball at any moment. The basic grip for a ready position has the left hand at the top of the stick and the right hand six to eight inches below the left hand. The *V*'s formed by the thumbs and fingers of both hands should point toward the toe of the stick. While running, the players carry the stick with the toe to the right of the body and as close to the ground as comfortable. While this position is basic, intermediate and advanced players may modify this carry as long as it does not hamper their playing the ball.

DRIBBLE

The dribble is a means of advancing the ball on the ground while maintaining possession of it. It is used in much the same manner as the dribble in soccer and basketball. A player should not dribble when she can pass, as the latter is a faster means of moving the ball. The player may also use one or two dribbles after fielding the ball to control it before passing.

The dribble consists of a series of taps of the ball in the direction the player is moving. Since *the ball may only be hit with the flat side of the stick,** the stick is turned

* Italics indicate rules that determine how skills may be performed.

with this side facing in the direction of the ball. The back of the left hand faces the ball, with the butt of the stick on the left side of the hand. The left forearm is parallel to the stick, with elbow high and the left shoulder in front of or leading the right

Fig. 4.5. Dribble

shoulder. These positions of the left hand, the arm, and the shoulder are crucial. The right hand is several inches down the stick to control the head of the stick. The more advanced the player, the closer her two

hands will be on the dribble. Beginners should place the right hand down far enough to control the toe of the stick but not farther than eight inches from the top hand. The ball is kept in front of the right foot. The dribbler reaches toward the ball with her left shoulder and arm and taps the ball forward with her left hand. The right hand provides control of the stick. The dribbler taps the ball far enough away to keep it away from her feet while running, yet in a position that is no more than one stride away from her stick. The faster the player runs, the harder she must tap the ball. A *loose* dribble may be used when a player is entirely free, although this rarely happens in the actual game. In this case, the ball is tapped farther ahead, and the player runs after it.

PROGRESSION AND TEACHING SUGGESTIONS

The most common errors in dribbling are:

1. Gripping the stick with the right hand well down the stick, causing an extreme crouched position for running.
2. Holding the stick on an angle to the right rather than perpendicular to the ground. This may be the result of holding the butt of the stick directly behind the wrist or even to the right of the hand or leading with the right shoulder rather than the left.
3. Playing the ball on the right side of the body, resulting in a crablike run or side step.
4. Hitting at the ball rather than tapping it.
5. Failing to reach with the left side to tap the ball, causing the ball to become entangled with the feet or causing the player to slow down.

6. Hitting the ball and running after it rather than maintaining control of the ball.

The dribble is a controlled stroke. Beginners are often anxious to see what it is like to hit the ball, since this may appear to be the primary object of having a stick. For this reason, it may be of value to let beginners experiment with a stick and ball, letting them hit the ball any way they wish, before introducing the dribble. It may even be valuable to introduce hitting and fielding the ball before the dribble to capitalize on this natural tendency of beginners.

Beginners seem to have difficulty with the position of the left arm and shoulder. Since most players are right-handed, they will tend to reach for the ball with the right arm. This places the stick on an angle back from the ball and makes the contact and control difficult. Reaching with the left shoulder and carrying the left elbow high must be emphasized so that players do not collapse the left elbow in close to the body.

DRILLS

Since field hockey requires speed and agility, good footwork should be encouraged from the beginning. Some of the following drills emphasize short, quick steps in various directions, as well as practice in dribbling.

1. Spread out on the field, each player carrying the stick in correct position with the correct grip moves as fast as possible to the left, right, front, or back, on command.

2. Spread out on the field, each player with a ball attempts to dribble the ball. While they may run slowly in the beginning, gamelike speed should be achieved quickly even if some control of the ball is lost.

3. In twos, approximately fifteen yards apart, one player dribbles, as quickly as possible, out and around her partner and back to place. The ball is rolled to the partner who then performs. Each time, the player should alternate the side she goes around.

4. If a relay is used, players must be required to tap the ball a given number of times within a specific distance. Otherwise, players will hit and run in an attempt to win the race.

FIELDING THE BALL

Fielding the ball from all angles, with the ball traveling at various speeds, is one of the most important aspects of the game. Each player on the team is called upon to perform this skill during the game. Seldom must a player stop the ball "dead"; rather, she must be able to intercept the path of the ball with her stick and maintain possession of it.

Fielding a ball coming directly toward the player from in front is much like fielding a ground ball in softball. The player gets in line with the path of the ball, moves forward, and extends the flat side of the stick to meet the ball. As in the dribble, it is important that the left shoulder lead in the reach to keep the stick perpendicular to the ground. The faster the ball is moving, the greater the potential rebound off the stick on contact. In order to maintain possession of the ball, the rebound must be minimal. Therefore, the faster the ball is moving, the greater the reach with the left arm. This creates a forward angle of the stick and the ground, forming a "pocket" to trap the ball. This may be accompanied with a slight "give" of the stick, being careful not to let the ball get too close to the feet.

When the ball is approaching from the player's left, she must allow the ball to travel across in front of her body before controlling it. It is imperative that her feet are pointed in the direction she ultimately wishes to go. If the ball is moving slowly, she should move toward the ball, circle to the right, and get her feet pointed in the direction she wishes to go before touching the ball. If the ball is moving rapidly, she may maintain her position, facing the flat side of the stick toward the oncoming ball, gather it in front of her right foot, and progress forward with it.

When the ball is approaching from the player's right, she must intercept the path of the ball before it crosses her body. The

Fig. 4.6. Fielding the ball

From the right　　　　　　　　　　　　　　　　From the left

flat side of the stick points toward the ball, and the feet are pointed downfield. As the angle of the approach of the ball increases, the player must rotate the upper half of her body in order to field the ball.

Balls approaching the player from the rear on either side require an extreme twist to the side of the ball with the upper half of the body. Players will find this twist more difficult on the right than on the left.

PROGRESSION AND TEACHING SUGGESTIONS

The most common errors in fielding the ball are:

1. Fielding the ball too close to the feet rather than reaching for the ball.
2. Not going to meet the ball when possible.
3. Pointing the feet in the direction of the ball rather than in the direction the player plans to go with the ball.
4. Hitting at the ball rather than "gathering" it in and going on with it.

The concept of gathering the ball in and either dribbling or passing is difficult for beginners. The natural tendency is to hit at the ball to interrupt its path. This can result in a complete miss of the ball, an inaccurate deflection, or the loss of possession because the ball is too far off the stick. The player must gauge the speed and direction of the ball as it is being hit and move accordingly. Some players find it helpful to point the toe of the stick toward the ball as it approaches in order to help line it up. Players must be able to cope with every conceivable angle of pass when the ball is traveling at various speeds. Drills should include as many variations as practical.

DRILLS

1. In twos, one player rolls the ball to another player who runs to meet the ball, fields it, and takes two dribbles forward. This may begin with balls coming from straight ahead, then from various angles. The roll should vary in speed and angle, with some balls approaching the player from directly behind.
2. Many combinations of drills can be used to practice fielding in conjunction with other skills. For example, player one rolls the ball to player two who fields the ball and dribbles around players three and four and back to player one. As more skills are presented (e.g., hit, dodge), the variations become endless for combination, gamelike drills.

QUICK HIT OR PASS

The quick hit is simply hitting the ball from the dribbling position. It differs from the drive in that the two hands are apart on the hit, rather than together. Since the "hands apart" hit has become a recognized skill of advanced players and since beginners tend to forget to bring their hands together for the drive, it is recommended that the quick hit be taught to beginners at this point.

The hands grip the stick approximately six inches apart, as in the dribble. For a hit to the left, the ball should be in front of the right foot. The player brings the stick directly back in a line opposite from the intended direction of the hit. The stick is taken back with two hands, the right hand lifting higher than the left to about waist height. *It is a foul to raise any part of the stick above the shoulder at any time.* For a quick hit players should be encouraged

Fig. 4.7. Quick hit

not to raise the toe of the stick much above -waist level. On the downswing and through contact of the ball, the player's right hand dominates the stroke, and the head is over the ball. At contact, she should feel as if she is hitting through the ball with her right hand. This is similar to batting a ball in softball. After contact, the toe of the stick remains low in the direction of the hit. The wrists should not be allowed to collapse upward, resulting in the toe of the stick rising high in the follow-through.

For a hit straight ahead, the ball is positioned slightly to the right of the right foot. The upper body, with shoulders leading, is rotated to the right. The stick is taken directly back, and the swing forward is in the direction of the hit.

For a hit to the right, the ball must be to the right and opposite the rear foot. The player must make a full twist of the upper body so that the shoulders are at right angles to the hips. The stick is brought directly back behind the body in a line opposite the direction of the hit. The forward swing is in the direction of the hit. Some players may find it easier to rotate their shoulders if the stick makes a slight outward and backward circle in preparation for the hit.

The analysis of the quick hit assumes that the player is moving as the ball is hit. If she is stationary, as in a free hit or corner hit, she may position her feet to hit the easier left hit in any direction. No mention has been made of the position of the feet on the hit. While it will be more comfortable to hit the ball while taking a step with the left foot in the direction of the hit, players should be encouraged to hit off either foot while maintaining their forward direction.

PROGRESSION AND TEACHING SUGGESTIONS

The most common errors in the quick hit are:

1. Playing the ball too far away, resulting in a sweeping outward stroke or undercut on the hit rather than a direct back and through stroke.
2. Raising the stick high on the backswing from too great a cocking of the wrists or from the assumption that the greater the backswing the harder the hit.
3. Failing to uncock the wrists, primarily the right wrist, at contact.
4. Following through upward rather than a short follow-through forward.

The quick hit is primarily a wrist stroke. It is a chopping hit at the ball as opposed to a swinging hit. Players should be encouraged to hit the ball as quickly as possible from the very beginning. This negates a long backswing as a part of the stroke. Strong wrist action caused by the right hand will give greater power in the drive as well.

DRILLS

1. In twos, approximately ten to fifteen yards apart, players quickly hit the ball back and forth as soon as it is received. Players should not hit the ball without first controlling it. The tempo should be control—hit, control—hit.
2. The drills indicated for practice in fielding the ball may now be used with a hit between two or more players rather than a roll.
3. In twos, threes, fours, and later fives, players move down the field, passing the ball and ending with a shot for goal. This approximates forward line play.
4. Various combination drills approximating gamelike situations can be devised. For example, groups of four players work together, one positioned as a fullback, one as a halfback, and two as forwards. The fullback has the ball and hits up to the halfback who, in turn, hits to either forward. The two forwards then move down the field and shoot for goal.

FIRST GAME SITUATION

With the direct interaction of players on the field, the first game situation can be confusing for the players. For this reason, unless the players have had experience with and understand the game of soccer, it is recommended that play begin with six- or seven-player teams on a reduced-size field. The positions and general strategy of field hockey are very similar to that of soccer, but players often have difficulty in making the transfer. Six-player field hockey can utilize one half of a regulation hockey field. The regulation center and goal lines act as sidelines and the sidelines as goal lines. Goals can be marked with pinnies or towels.

Each team consists of three forwards and three defense. If a seventh player is added, she acts as a backup defense. Instructions should be kept to a minimum, with rules and basic strategy introduced as the situations occur.

Some basic restrictions need to be given prior to play for the safety of the players. For example, it is a foul to raise any part of the stick above the shoulders at any time; no more than two opposing players should attempt to play the ball at one time, all others should pull away to avoid creating a "mess"; do not hit directly into an opponent; try to *take* the ball away rather than slashing at it. Very basic strategy should be stressed: Each defense player is responsible for a specific opposing forward and must be between her opponent and the goal when the opposing team has the ball; Defense play behind their forwards, passing the ball and following them down the field, always ready to reposition in case their team loses the ball; Forwards attempt to move the ball down the field with a series of passes and hit the ball into the goal; Forwards should maintain their relative positions of left, center, and right.

Play begins with one team in possession of the ball in the center of the field and all other players at least five yards away. Since this is the same as a free hit, it can then be utilized in the event of a foul later in play. Players should be allowed to play, within safety restrictions, and work out their own problems without too much interference in the beginning. Care must be taken not to interrupt the game continuously unless it gets "bogged" down. Obstruction, advancing, and bunching of players will occur and should be mentioned, but play need not be stopped with each infraction unless it threatens the safety of the players.

As play continues, defense hits, roll-ins, and further strategy can be introduced. It is recommended that time be allotted for discussion by the players. This discussion should point out the need for dodges, tackles, and other techniques.

Once the players have experienced the six-player game, progression to the regulation game should be made as soon as possible. Players should be encouraged to try a variety of positions. The regulation game employs the same restrictions with ten players on a side. It is not recommended that players be placed in the goal until they have had some instruction and are properly protected.

Intermediate Skills

Intermediate skills are vital to the game, although a basic regulation game can be played with just the beginning skills.

STRAIGHT TACKLE

The straight tackle is a means of taking the ball away from an opponent when the opponent is approaching directly toward the tackler. The tackler, with her stick low, the flat side facing the ball, moves toward the player who has the ball. The tackle is timed so that the stick is placed against the ball when the ball is off the opponent's stick. The tackler holds her stick as if she were fielding a ball coming directly toward her. The right hand is six to eight inches down the stick in a strong position, and the left shoulder leads, putting the stick at a forward angle to trap the ball. The tackler is in a stationary forward stride position with the ball trapped, while the dribbler's forward momentum should carry her past the

Fig. 4.8. Straight tackle

trapped ball. The tackler then quickly passes or dribbles the ball in the direction of her goal.

PROGRESSION AND TEACHING SUGGESTIONS

The most common errors in performing the straight tackle are:

1. Flinging or slashing the stick at the ball rather than placing it firmly.
2. Not leading with the left shoulder and forming a backward angle of the stick, permitting the ball to roll over or up the stick.
3. Mistiming the tackle; contacting the ball when it is on the opponent's stick.

No tackle is a "sure" thing. If a tackle were always successful, there would be no game. Tackling is a one-on-one situation in which both offense and defense should be playing "cat and mouse." The tackler's objectives are to slow the dribbler down, force her to pass, or successfully tackle. Since the dribbler will learn how to dodge a potential tackler, the timing of the tackle is crucial. The position of the tackler is generally slightly to the left of the oncoming player so as to be in a stick-to-stick relationship. However, this position may vary if the dribbler is known to always dodge to one side or if the players are close to goal. In the latter situation, the defensive player positions slightly to the goal side of the dribbler, forcing her to dodge away from goal. The tackler does not just rush headlong at the dribbler, hoping the ball will be off the stick when she arrives. Rather, she moves quickly, watching the dribbler and timing her tackle at the most advantageous moment. If the dribbler loses control of the ball or is dribbling loosely, the ball may be taken away by simply pulling or pushing the ball to one side, and no tackle is necessary.

Beginners, in the heat of the game, will tend to slash their sticks at the ball in the hope this will get the ball away from the opponent. At this point the game is no longer field hockey and may cause injuries, or at least cause some players to decide

that this isn't the game for them. *It is illegal to strike, hook, hit, hold, or interfere in any way with an opponent's stick.*

DRILLS

In twos, one player dribbles at top speed toward the other; the second player attempts a straight tackle. In the beginning, this may be performed at less than top speed in order to make sure all players understand the concept of the tackle, but it should be performed at game speed as soon as possible. The timing of the tackle is quite different when the dribbler is walking and running.

Fig. 4.9. Left dodge

Further practice in the straight tackle should wait until the left and right dodges are introduced.

LEFT AND RIGHT DODGES

A dodge is a means of evading a potential tackler while maintaining possession of the ball. When a tackler is approaching the dribbler for a straight tackle, the dribbler may dodge to the left or right. In either case, the dribbler must conceal until the last moment which dodge she will use by continuing directly at the opponent. More advanced players may deliberately veer to one side as a deceptive maneuver, but beginners tend to veer in the direction of the intended dodge.

The left dodge is executed just as the tackler is about to tackle. The ball is pulled at a ninety-degree angle to the left, just out of reach of the tackler's stick. With the pull, the dodger's feet must quickly move with short steps to the left. As soon as the tackler's stick is cleared, the dodger immediately and quickly dribbles forward, clear of the tackler. This dodge is also called the pull-to-the-left dodge and, because of the pattern of the path of the ball, the "staircase" dodge.

The right dodge is also executed just as the tackler is about to tackle. The ball is

pushed on a diagonal path to the right of the tackler on her "nonstick" side. The ball is pushed just far enough to clear the tackler. The dodger quickly goes to the left and picks up the ball behind the tackler. The dodger may not follow the ball to the right, as she would obstruct the tackler. *It is illegal to run between an opponent and the ball, prohibiting her from playing the ball.*

PROGRESSION AND TEACHING SUGGESTIONS

The most common errors in dodging are:

1. Slowing down as the tackler approaches.
2. Veering to the side of intended dodge.
3. Beginning the dodge too soon or too late.

4. Dodging too wide, permitting the tackler to reposition for a tackle, or losing possession of the ball.

In an attempt to be very accurate in the stick work required for a dodge, many players slow down prior to executing the skill. In actuality, this accomplishes one of the objectives of the tackler, namely, to slow the dribbler down. To counteract the tendency to slow down, players should be instructed to speed up when about to dodge. A sudden burst of speed may also catch the tackler by surprise. The dodger must be aware that the tackler may fake a tackle to confuse the dribbler and cause her to commit herself to a dodge too soon. The dodger

must watch the tackler and not have her eyes solely on the ball. Many players find that they prefer one dodge over another. A good defense player will detect this and play for that particular dodge.

A player should not attempt a dodge if a pass will be more effective. She must be aware, however, that the second objective of a potential tackler is to *force* a pass. A forced pass implies that the dribbler is hurried and passing to get rid of the ball. This usually results in an inaccurate pass that may be intercepted, or it may slow the attacking move down. Therefore, the player with the ball must be aware of the options and the positions of players on both teams each time she receives the ball.

DRILLS

1. Players spread on the field, each with a ball, dribble left, right, back, and forward on command or on their own. This must be done at game speed.

2. In twos, ten to fifteen yards apart, player with ball dribbles toward partner and attempts left or right dodge as partner attempts straight tackle. This should approximate game speed.

3. In groups of six, three offense versus three defense, the offense, dribbling, dodging, and passing, attempts to move the ball from one side of the field to the other.

Fig. 4.10. Right dodge

DRIVE

The drive is a means of hitting the ball moderate to long distances. It is used as a pass, as a shot, on free hits, corner hits, and defense hits. It differs from the quick hit in that the right hand is brought up to the left before contact. This increase in lever length should permit greater force in hitting the ball.

The swing and hit are basically the same as the quick hit. The ball may be a few inches farther away from the player be-

cause of the increased length of the stick. On the backswing, the arms should be free of the body, and the right wrist cocks back. The left wrist should be kept fairly firm to prevent the possibility of raising the stick above the shoulders on the backswing. On contact, the right hand should hit through the ball, causing the right wrist to snap forward. The head should be over the ball at contact. The follow-through, with firm wrists, is low, in the direction of the hit.

PROGRESSION AND TEACHING SUGGESTIONS

The most common errors in performing the drive are:

1. Failing to bring the hands together.
2. Losing control of the head of the stick when the right hand is moved up the stick.
3. Overcocking the wrists on backswing and follow-through.
4. Failing to hit through the ball with the right hand, resulting in a loss of power.

Some beginning players find it difficult to control the head of the stick with the hands together at the top of the stick. This may be due to a lack of strength, too long or too heavy a stick, or too loose a grip. At any rate, if players lose control of the stick, weak inaccurate hits will result. If it is a lack of basic strength, the player should continue with the quick hit (hands apart) until such time as she can control the drive. In the excitement of the game, players can become wild with their sticks and dan-

Fig. 4.11. Drive

gerous to players around them. Control of the stick, therefore, is paramount from the beginning, and wild, uncontrolled play should be stopped whenever it occurs.

DRILLS

The drills indicated for the quick hit may be used for practice of the drive. In addition, it is recommended that players practice hitting the ball as far as they can. It is very difficult to hit the ball long and hard if the basic technique is incorrect.

BULLY

The bully is taken by center forwards at the beginning of each half, after each goal, and when the offense fouls in a penalty bully. All other players may be required to bully in the instance of a double foul or in a penalty bully.

The bully is taken by two players, *each squarely facing the sideline with her goal line to her right. Each player hits the ground on her side of the ball and her opponent's stick over the ball alternately, each three*

Fig. 4.12. Bully—beginning position

times. After the third hit of sticks, the ball is in play. Only the flat side of the stick may make contact with the opponent's stick. The two players should grip their sticks in a strong position with right hand six to eight inches down. The weight is over the balls of the feet, the feet approximately ten inches apart. The knees are flexed, and the head is over the ball. The objective of each player in the bully is to direct the ball to a teammate at its conclusion. Therefore, each player tries to get her stick quickly on the

ball after the third hit of sticks. There are three basic maneuvers that can be attempted: push to the left, hit to the right, and lift over opponent's stick.

The push or hit to the left begins with the player pulling the ball toward herself, moving her feet backward. As soon as the ball is clear of her opponent's stick, the player pushes or hits the ball to the left, being careful not to interpose her right shoulder between her opponent and the ball and thus cause obstruction.

Fig. 4.13. Pull-to-left bully

The hit to the right begins with the player turning her stick over into a reverse stick position. This is accomplished by sliding the right hand clockwise around the stick until the palm faces up. The stick is then turned within the left hand until the palm of the right hand faces down and the flat side of the stick faces to the right. This turning of the stick is accomplished in one quick motion. The reverse stick is placed on the left side of the ball, and the ball is drawn directly back about eighteen inches. At this point, the stick is taken back to the regular position as the player takes a short backswing and hits the ball to the right behind her opponent.

Lifting over an opponent's stick can occur when both players have their sticks on either side of the ball and both are exerting pressure on the ball in opposing directions. Maintaining pressure on the ball, the player lifts her stick and the ball up and over the opponent's stick.

PROGRESSION AND TEACHING SUGGESTIONS

The most common errors in bullying are:

1. Holding the stick in a "weak" position with hands close together.
2. Failing to get the head over the ball and reaching with extended arms.
3. Locking the knees.
4. Not having a constructive plan and simply trying to hit the ball somewhere or slashing at the ball.

Pull back   Hit or push right

Fig. 4.14. Hit-to-right bully

Fig. 4.15. Lift-over-opponent's-stick bully

Fig. 4.16. Two-hand left tackle

DRILLS

Spread on the field in twos and using any of the lines available, players bully and attempt all of the various possibilities.

LEFT TACKLES

Left tackles are used when the tackler is chasing the opponent with the ball and the opponent is on her left. Right halfbacks and right fullbacks must be particularly skilled in left tackles, as these tackles place the defense on the goal side of an opponent. However, all players, including forwards, should be able to execute a left tackle.

There are two basic left tackles: the two-hand left tackle and the left-hand lunge.

The two-hand left tackle should be used whenever the opponent is close enough to be reached with two hands on the stick. The left-hand lunge is reserved for when the opponent can only be reached with a long stride and extension of the left hand on the top of the stick.

The two-hand left tackle requires no backswing. The tackler times the placing of her stick directly in front of the ball, interrupting its intended path, when the ball is off the dribbler's stick. At this point, the tackler quickly gets her feet around, pointed in the direction she wishes to go, and takes the ball away from her opponent.

The left-hand lunge is initiated when the tackler is one long stride away from and

behind the dribbler. The tackler should only use the left-hand lunge if it is imperative that the tackle be made immediately (e.g., the player is about to shoot), if the tackler cannot catch the dribbler, or if it will be a surprise maneuver. Otherwise, the two-hand left tackle should be employed. With two hands, the tackler takes the stick to her right side, keeping the stick low, in preparation for the lunge. As the tackler takes a long stride with her left foot toward the dribbler, the stick is swung out and around until the right hand can no longer remain on the stick. The left hand remains as the sole control of the stick as it is placed directly in front of the ball, interrupting the path of the ball. The tackler must quickly get her feet around and behind her stick and replace the right hand. The lunge is timed as the ball is off the opponent's stick.

PROGRESSION AND TEACHING SUGGESTIONS

The most common errors in performing left tackles are:

1. Using a lunge when a two-hand tackle is possible.
2. Hitting at the ball rather than placing the stick on the ball in a strong position.
3. Hitting the opponent's stick. This is a foul.
4. Beginning the lunge with a high back-swing, often to the point of committing sticks.

The two-hand left tackle is a basic tackle that is often neglected or forgotten in favor of the left-hand lunge. Many beginning players find it difficult to control the stick with one hand, and too many players at all levels use the left-hand lunge when a two-

Fig. 4.17. Left-hand lunge.

hand tackle would be more effective. It is strongly recommended that the two-hand left tackle be taught *before* the left-hand lunge. The left-hand lunge may even be deferred until after the players have become proficient in the two-hand tackle.

DRILLS

In twos, one player dribbles the ball at a moderate pace; the other player attempts a left tackle. The pace of the dribbler should be increased to game speed but not to the point where a faster runner simply outruns a slower opponent. Players should be matched by speed so this does not occur. At first, players simply take turns at tackling. Later, this can become a continuous drill in which the tackler immediately becomes the dribbler upon possession of the ball and the dribbler must tackle back. This is one method of combining conditioning with the practice of a skill.

RIGHT OR CIRCULAR TACKLE

The right or circular tackle is used when the tackler is chasing an opponent with the ball who is on her right. Left halfbacks and left fullbacks should be particularly proficient in this tackle as it positions them between their opponent and the goal. Because the rules prohibit placing the body between an opponent and the ball, a tackler may not simply reach to her right and draw the ball away. She must turn toward her opponent as she tackles. The tackler must draw even with or ahead of the dribbler before beginning the tackle. As the ball leaves the dribbler's stick, the tackler reaches with two hands to place her stick on the ball. If the ball is very close to the dribbler, the tackler may tap the ball slightly ahead. At this point, the tackler quickly moves her feet in a semicircle in front of the dribbler, her stick in contact with the ball making a smaller circle than her feet. The tackler moves around with the left shoulder leading well in front of her right shoulder. The semicircle should take the tackler *and* the ball across the path of the dribbler to the other side. The forward momentum of the dribbler should carry her past the ball. The tackler is now in position to dribble or pass.

PROGRESSION AND TEACHING SUGGESTIONS

The most common errors in performing the circular tackle are:

1. Failing to be even or slightly ahead of the opponent.

Fig. 4.18. Circular tackle

2. Interfering with the opponent's stick. This is a foul.
3. Not leading with the left shoulder, making it difficult to circle in front of the opponent.

The circular tackle is a difficult skill. It assumes that the tackler can outrun and circle in front of an opponent who is dribbling at top speed. It is not unusual to see players substituting a right jab for the circular tackle, even though the former is more of a "spoil" stroke than a tackle. If the dribbler tends to slow down as a tackler approaches, it makes any tackle easier.

In practice, players should be matched for speed, and the dribbler should move only at a moderate pace. There is no oppor-

tunity to practice a circular tackle if the tackler cannot catch the dribbler.

DRILLS

The same drills as indicated for the practice of the left tackles may be used for the circular tackle.

GOALKEEPING

Goalkeeping utilizes some unique techniques. Players should be familiar with these techniques and other requirements for goalkeeping before they are expected to play this position. *The goalkeeper is permitted to kick the ball, stop it with any part of her body, and allow it to rebound off her body or hand. It is a foul, called advancing,*

if any other player propels the ball in any manner other than with her stick. In order to kick the ball or allow it to rebound off her legs, the goalkeeper should be protected with leg guards and kickers or boots.

The goalkeeper positions in front of the goal line. She moves on an imaginary semicircular line drawn from goal post to goal post, depending on the position of the ball. As the ball approaches, the goalkeeper gets in line with the hit, using a side-stepping movement with feet close together. At the impact of the ball, her feet are together and knees are slightly bent to cause the ball to rebound to the ground in front of her feet. After the ball is stopped or deflected, it is cleared to the nearest sideline. The clear is executed with the inside of the foot away from the sideline, using a short side-swing of the leg. The goalkeeper must be able to

Fig. 4.19. Goalkeeper   Preparing to block the ball   Clearing the ball

use either foot with equal facility to clear. Although the goalkeeper must carry a stick, it is only used when the ball cannot be reached with her feet. The stick is usually carried in the right hand. The hand grips the stick approximately six to eight inches down the grip.

DRILLS

Since it is not practical to have goal pads and kickers for a great number of players, it is recommended that general practice in goalkeeping be conducted using tennis or small rubber balls.

In twos, each twosome is given five to six tennis balls and two pinnies or towels. The pinnies are placed approximately four yards apart on a line on the field. One player takes the position of goalkeeper while the other stands about ten yards away with the tennis balls. The tennis balls are rolled on the ground toward the goalkeeper by hand. The goalkeeper positions for each roll, controls the ball, and clears to the nearest sideline. In the beginning, the balls should be rolled directly at the goalkeeper. As practice progresses, the balls can be rolled faster, from varying angles and to one side of the goalkeeper.

If a few extra sets of leg guards and kickers are available, players waiting on the sidelines during a game can practice goalkeeping and shooting while two players have the actual experience in the game.

PUSH PASS

The push pass is just what its name implies. The ball is pushed along the ground with the stick. The push pass is effective as a short pass because it requires no backswing and can be deceptive.

With left shoulder leading, the player places the stick behind the ball at a ninety-degree angle. The ball is pushed in the intended direction, the stick remaining in contact with the ball as long as possible. The follow-through is low, in the direction of the pass.

DRILLS

Drills indicated for other passes may be used for the push pass. In addition, players may get the "feel" of pushing rather than hitting if a soccer ball is used instead of a hockey ball.

ROLL-IN

Although the primary concern of a roll-in is strategic in nature, the roll itself may be considered a technique.

The player executing a roll-in is positioned *outside the sideline. Her feet and stick must remain behind the line until the ball is released. The ball may not be bounced or thrown and must touch the ground within one yard of the point where it initially crossed the sideline in going out of bounds.* The roller may roll the ball hard and long close to the sideline, short to a cutting player, or even backwards on the field. The basic forward roll-in is executed with knees well bent but not touching the ground. From this low position, the arm sweeps forward with an underhand motion, releasing the ball just off the ground. The fingers should extend toward the ground in the direction of the roll so that the ball does not loft into the air. Rolling the ball backward is usually preceded by a deceptive feint as if the player were going to roll the ball forward. Instead of releasing the ball on the forward swing, the player

Fig. 4.20. Roll-in

turns her hand and rolls the ball to the side or back.

DRILLS

The roll-in should be practiced in a game-like situation. Although used primarily by side halfbacks, all players should practice the roll-in since beginners will be playing a variety of positions.

The first practice can be in groups of four. One player takes the roll-in, another is positioned as a wing down the field, another as an inner about ten yards from the alley, and the last as a fullback to the rear of the roller on the field. The roller practices rolling to all three players. Players rotate as does the direction of the roll. Players rolling on the left side of the field should use their right hand to roll; when on the right, they use their left hand. Later, a halfback opposing the wing should

be added, then an opposing wing and inner.

Selected Advanced Skills

Advanced skills may or may not be included in an instructional class, depending on the ability and interest of the students.

SCOOP

The scoop is a means of putting the ball into the air over short distances. It may be used as a pass, shot, or dodge.

To execute a scoop, the player extends the stick toward the ball at a low angle, approximately thirty degrees, to the ground. The flat side of the stick faces up, with the right and left hands shifted slightly to the left on the grip. In this position, the toe of the stick is placed against the ball, and the right hand lifts up and

Fig. 4.21. Scoop

forward, causing the ball to lift into the air. As a dodge, the ball need only be lifted a few inches off the ground to clear the opponent's stick. As a pass or shot, it may be lifted higher for greater distance, provided it is not dangerous to another player.

Since the scoop is usually executed on the run, it is suggested that the left hand be slightly to the left side of the body. This will prevent the player from impaling herself on the stick should it hit a tuft of grass or dig into the ground.

FLICK

The flick is another means of putting the ball into the air. The flick can be more effective over longer distances than the scoop and is more deceptive since it can be executed faster. The flick is initiated by placing the stick against the ball as in the push pass. Some players find it helpful to start with the stick on the right of the ball and move the stick behind the ball as a part of the total stroke. The ball is pushed forward with a strong right-hand action,

allowing the stick to lay back on the push. As the stick lays back, it will be beneath the ball, and a continued push causes the ball to lift off the ground. At this point, the ball is still on the stick, and the player gives further impetus to the ball by flicking her wrists—the left wrist to the right, the right wrist to the left. Short, quick flicks can be executed from a slightly crouched position. However, long, forceful flicks require that the player be low and take a step, usually with the left leg. At the completion of the stroke, the player's right knee will be close to the ground.

JAB

The jab is an emergency spoiling stroke used when a tackle is not possible at that moment. It is a one-handed reaching stroke that attempts to poke the ball away from an opponent. It may be attempted from various angles but is usually employed when the dribbler is about to shoot or pass and the tackler is behind. If the dribbler is

From left

From right

Fig. 4.23. Jab

on the left, the tackler's left hand is at the top of the stick for greatest reach. If the dribbler is on the right, the tackler's right hand is moved to the top of the stick. With one hand, the stick is extended toward the ball one or more times in an attempt to move the ball to the far side of the dribbler. The jab can direct the ball to a nearby teammate, past the dribbler, and the tackler recovers the ball; or it can simply slow down the play and the dribbler. It must be remembered that the jab most often is a spoiling of the action and not necessarily a tackle. Players should not use a jab when a more reliable tackle is possible.

REVERSE STICK PLAY

Since field hockey can only be played right-handed and the ball hit with the flat side of the stick, there are occasions when a player may turn her stick over to play the ball. This is called a reverse stick.

A *reverse stick hit* allows a player to hit the ball to the right without rotating her shoulders and upper body. Prior to the hit, the grip is reversed as shown in figure 4.24a. This is accomplished by sliding the right hand under the stick and turning the stick counterclockwise, allowing it to rotate within the left hand. The ball is in front of the right foot and is hit to the right with a short backswing and follow-through.

A *reverse stick dodge* to the right is performed in the same manner as the basic left dodge. The stick is reversed and the ball pulled at a ninety-degree angle to the right to clear the opponent. The player then is in position to dribble straight ahead. The player must be aware of the possibility of the foul obstruction when using this dodge.

STRATEGY

The team with the ball is on offense; the team without the ball is on defense. Field hockey requires the direct interaction of two teams of eleven players each.

The official game consists of two thirty-five-minute halves with no substitution except for injury unless modified rules are used allowing substitution at half time. Each goal counts one point. Each team at-tempts to score as many goals as possible and to prevent the opposing team from scoring. It is toward these ends that all field hockey strategy is aimed.

Basic strategy for offense and defense is presented in this section. Basic strategy is essential to *all* levels of play.

Offensive Strategy

The game begins with a center bully. Neither team has possession of the ball until the bully is completed and the ball has been directed toward a player. At this

a. Grip   b

Fig. 4.24. Reverse stick hit.

point both teams are positioned as in figure 4.25. The forwards should cross the line with the third hit of sticks on the bully in anticipation of a pass. The general strategy on offense is to avoid the cluster of players in the middle of the field between the two twenty-five-yard lines by passing to the wings. Once inside the opponent's twenty-five-yard line, the ball is centered for the attempt to score. The team on offense attempts to get free from their opposing defense and take the ball to their opponent's goal by dribbling, dodging, and passing. While play in midfield is important, the object of the game is to score a goal.

Because of the *off side rule,* players on the forward line cannot wait downfield near the opponent's goal for the ball. The five forwards are often called the forward "line" since they tend to advance down the field in a line across the field in their respective positions. The halfbacks on the offensive team follow and back up the forward line, not allowing a gap of more than ten to fifteen yards between them and the forwards. One fullback remains in a cover-

ing position; the other joins the forwards and halfbacks on offense.

Once the ball crosses the opponent's twenty-five-yard line and forwards enter the striking circle, all attention is centered on the goal. *Shooting* for goal is simply accurate passing to elude the opponents and goalkeeper.

If the defensive team unintentionally sends the ball over their own goal line, not between the goalposts, a *corner* is awarded the offensive team. The corner hit is taken five yards from the corner of the field. Players line up as in figure 4.26. The objective on the corner is to direct the ball to a forward on the edge of the striking circle who then *controls* the ball (stopping it but not necessarily motionless) and immediately shoots for goal. The forwards on the edge of the circle wait for a well-hit ball rather than running to meet it, since the ball can travel faster than the onrushing defense. This permits the forward a free second in which to shoot. As in all shots for goal, at least two other forwards should rush toward the goal on the shot, ready to

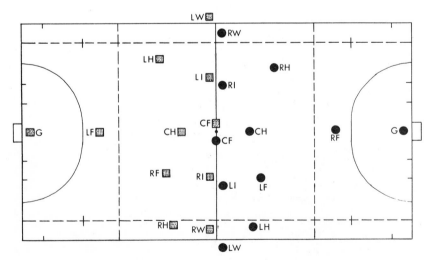

Fig. 4.25. Lineup for center bully.

play the ball if it should rebound off the goalkeeper. The majority of goals in field hockey are scored on second and even third shots by rushing forwards. The procedure and positioning for the *penalty corner* is the same as in the corner except that the hit is taken from a point not less than ten yards from the goalpost.

A *free hit* may occur at virtually any point on the field. Free hits are awarded for fouls by the opposing team and to the defensive team when the offensive team has sent the ball over the end line. There are some differences in strategy, depending on where the free hit is taken. When a free hit is awarded behind the twenty-five-yard line, the player taking the free hit should avoid hitting into the center of the field or across her goal. An attempt should be made to hit the ball long and hard toward the nearest wing or inner. Between the two twenty-five-yard lines, there is greater flexibility on the direction of the

free hit. The player taking the free hit attempts to hit the ball directly to a free player or into a space where a player can run and receive the ball. When inside the opponent's twenty-five-yard line, the free hit is taken so that a teammate can immediately shoot for goal upon receiving the hit.

The general strategy for the *roll-in* is mentioned in the skills section. The wing positioned for the roll-in down the sideline cuts toward the sideline as the ball is released. The inner, positioned approximately five yards away from the five-yard line and on line or slightly ahead of the roller, also must cut toward the ball rolled toward her. The fullback positioned behind the roller near the five-yard line must be very alert and usually directs her hit across the field should the roll-in come to her.

Different positions require special abilities. The following briefly summarizes some of these abilities for the team on the offense.

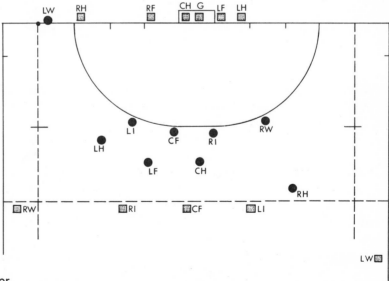

Fig. 4.26. Lineup for corner

Left Wing

Fielding the ball from the right
Right drive or hit for centering and passing the ball
Smooth, hard hit on corner

Left Inner

Fielding the ball from the right more than from the left
Right drive or hit more than left
Good shots of varying types

Center Forward

Ability to move in small spaces with and without the ball
Good shots of varying types
Drive or hit equally to left and right
Fielding the ball equally from right and left

Right Inner

Fielding the ball from left more than right
Left drive or hit more than right
Good shots of varying types

Right Wing

Fielding the ball from the left
Left drive or hit for centering or passing ball
Smooth, hard hit on corner

All forwards must be able to run quickly over moderate distances and must be in condition to continue this action. The wings generally have bigger spaces within which to field the ball, dribble, and pass. The wings may have more opportunities to utilize the "loose" dribble with relative freedom. The inner and center forwards operate in a more confined area with many other players close by. The three inside forwards have the responsibility for rushing the goal on shots.

Halfbacks

Backing up the forwards, yet ready to go on defense, demanding speed and endurance
Shooting from edge of the circle when the opportunity presents itself
Side halfbacks required to take the roll in
All halfbacks take free hits requiring good drive or pass

Fullbacks

Clearing ball quickly to forwards to start the offense
One fullback joins halfbacks in backing up forwards, demanding speed and endurance
Good hard drive for free hits

Goalkeeper

Clears ball quickly toward sideline to initiate offense

GENERAL OFFENSIVE STRATEGY

1. Players should try to position with feet pointed toward the opponent's goal at all times.
2. Pass *to* a free player and into a space to a marked player.
3. Players should not stand still to receive the ball, but should move to receive it.
4. The game requires that players keep repositioning.
5. The object of the game is to score goals. Halfbacks and fullbacks should contribute by backing up and feeding passes to the forwards.

Defensive Strategy

Defensive strategy begins with the center bully. As soon as the bully is completed, one team is on the defense. The first concept of defensive strategy is that of *marking* an opponent. Marking implies that the defensive player is between her opponent and the goal, usually on the ball side, in a position to intercept a pass directed at her opponent. This implies that the defensive player is within a stick's length of her opponent. Should her opponent get the ball, the defensive player is in position to tackle. Although the entire team without the ball is on the defensive, halfbacks and fullbacks are specifically defense players since they are responsible for marking the opposing forwards. The side halfbacks mark the wings, the center halfback marks the center forward, and the fullbacks mark the inners.

Since it is possible for a forward to dodge her opponent or to get between her opponent and goal, a system allowing another defense player to pick up the free player is necessary. This system is called *covering*. All defense players are involved in covering except the center halfback. The center halfback might be referred to as the pivot of the defense since she always remains with the center forward except in extreme emergency. The positioning for covering is determined by the position of the ball. Covering operates on the theory that the forward farthest away from the ball is the least dangerous. For example, if the right wing has the ball, the left halfback is marking or attempting to tackle. The left fullback is marking the right inner. The right halfback moves in to cover the left inner, freeing the right fullback who moves back toward the goal to cover for a free player or a pass across the field. Therefore, the left or right fullback is back at all times, and one side halfback is marking an inner, depending on the position of the

ball. This positioning is maintained by the defense even when they have possession of the ball, as seen in figure 4.26 showing the lineup for the corner. This enables a team to shift effectively from offense to defense. As the ball is passed from one side of the field to the other, the fullbacks may either switch their up and back positions or the up fullback may move from side to side with the ball if this can be done without getting behind the play.

The defensive team on a *corner* is lined up as shown in figure 4.26. The rules require that six players be behind the end line. On the corner hit, the defense players run as quickly as possible to a stick-to-stick position with their respective opponents. When play is very close to the goal, *all* defense players mark their opponents.

Defending against a free hit requires the cooperation of the entire defensive team, both forwards and defense. The closest three forwards form a semicircle five yards away from the player taking the free hit in an attempt to block the direction of the ball. The defense players mark their respective opponents on the goal side.

On a *roll-in*, the defensive forwards attempt to block out the opposing forwards by positioning between them and the roll-in. The defending defense players mark their opponents on the goal side.

Forwards on the defending team should tackle back on opposing players when they initially lose the ball. Once the opposing forwards are in possession of the ball and the defending defense players are attempting to tackle, the defending forwards should position in anticipation for a pass should their defense gain possession of the ball. Defending forwards generally do not go back into their own striking circle to "help" their defense. This tends to cause confusion, and the forwards are not ready to begin the offense should their team get the ball.

There are a variety of positions that defending forwards can assume when the ball is deep in their defending area of the field. The *W*-formation places the wings and the center forward well down the field. The inners are back to pick up short clears from the defense and direct them to the wings or center forward. This is an aggressive positioning and requires that the defense be able to make long clears or passes to the wings and that the inners be able to pick up short clears yet catch the forward line at the other end of the field in time to shoot. The collapsed *W*-formation adjusts with the ball, bringing the wing on the ball side back when the defense is having difficulty in making long clears. In each case, the object is to clear the ball in such a way that several free forwards can advance the ball down the field.

Different positions require particular abilities. The following briefly summarizes some of these abilities for the team on defense.

Forwards

Tackle back immediately upon losing the ball
Reposition for the switch from defense to offense

Left Halfback

Circular or right tackle
Roll in with right hand
Speed and endurance

Center Halfback

Operate within confined area
Distribute play to left and right

Right Halfback

Left tackle
Roll in with left hand
Speed and endurance

Left Fullback

Circular or right tackle
Accurate hard hit

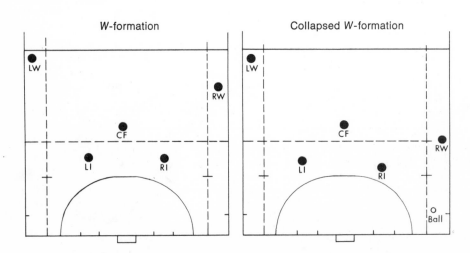

Fig. 4.27. Forwards on defense.

Right Fullback

Left tackle
Accurate hard hit

Goalkeeper

Courage
Quick reaction and movement time
Agility

GENERAL DEFENSIVE STRATEGY

1. When marking, each player should mark closely.
2. Players must be able to switch quickly from defense to offense.
3. When switching from marking to covering, players should move quickly and decisively.
4. The object of the defense is first to secure the ball and second to prevent their opponents from scoring.

BASIC UNIT PLAN FOR BEGINNERS

The following eighteen lessons represent a guide for the instruction of beginners. Each teaching situation is unique, however, and units should be developed based on the needs of the particular group of learners. It is assumed that some type of warm-up will precede each lesson. It is suggested that warm-ups include basic elements of the game. It is further assumed that review of previously presented skills will occur, based on student performance. Practice stations can be used periodically or as warm-ups. These stations can include tasks of a skills test nature. Officiating, rules, and strategy are best developed as situations occur in the game situation and skills presentations. However, time is allotted for general discussion and instruction in these areas. Whenever possible, each lesson should include game or gamelike situations.

Lesson 1	Grip and carry, dribble, fielding
Lesson 2	Fielding, quick hit, passing
Lesson 3	Game situation
Lesson 4	Straight tackle, left and right dodge
Lesson 5	Basic defense—play
Lesson 6	Basic offense—play
Lesson 7	Drive, bully—play
Lesson 8	Left tackles, right tackles
Lesson 9	Practice stations—play
Lesson 10	Goalkeeping—play
Lesson 11	Push pass, roll-in
Lesson 12	Corners—play
Lesson 13	Free hits—play
Lesson 14	Play—officiating
Lesson 15–18	Tournament play

SELECTED BIBLIOGRAPHY

BARNES, MILDRED J. *Field Hockey: The Coach and Player.* Boston: Allyn & Bacon, Inc., 1969.

DELANO, ANNE LEE. *Field Hockey.* Dubuque, Ia.: Wm Brown Co. Publishers, 1966.

DGWS. *Field Hockey–Lacrosse Guide.* Washington, D.C.: AAHPER. Published every two years.

HAUSSERMAN, CAROLINE. *Hockey for Beginners.* Boston: Allyn & Bacon, Inc., 1970.

MACKEY, HELEN. *Field Hockey: An International Team Sport.* Englewood Cliffs, N.J.: Prentice-Hall, Inc., 1963.

Lacrosse

Lacrosse is a team sport played primarily in the spring of the year in the United States. It is growing on the international level as well as in this country. Great Britain and Ireland are known for their high level of play, with emerging programs in Holland, France, Australia, and New Zealand, to name a few.

Lacrosse, played predominantly on the East Coast, is best known in the United States as a game for men. It has been referred to as the oldest organized sport in North America, as it originated with the American Indian of New York State and Ontario, Canada. The game was taken to England where it also developed as a game for women. American women were introduced to the game in the early 1900s by visiting English teachers. The United States Women's Lacrosse Association (USWLA) was formed in 1931, and in 1934 a team from England toured the country to assist with the spreading of the game. The first United States touring team played in Great Britain in 1951. Since that time, exchange tours of national teams occur approximately every three years.

Although the game is somewhat confined to the eastern coast of the United States, its growth and development have been seen over the years in various selected parts of the country. It is still known primarily as an "Eastern" game, however. One of the reasons for the lack of total development is the comparison with the men's game. Men's lacrosse is a body-contact sport often characterized as "rough." School administrators and teachers often equate women's lacrosse with men's and, therefore, not as a suitable activity for girls and women. The two games are very different, particularly in that body contact and rough, uncontrolled play are not permitted in the women's game. Other reasons for the lack of development are the apparent scarcity of qualified teachers and coaches and the already "crowded" spring schedule of sports activities.

Women's lacrosse is characterized by relative freedom from complicated and complex rules and by comparatively few different skills, yet the game permits skills and strategy that can be as demanding as the level of performance dictates.

The sole rule-making body in the United States is the USWLA in conjunction with a committee appointed by the DGWS. The rules are published every two years by the DGWS in the *Field Hockey–Lacrosse Guide*.

EQUIPMENT

Balls

The lacrosse ball may be any color, although white is most common in the United States. It is a hard rubber ball with a solid center which causes it to bounce off a hard surface and, in general, be more lively than balls used in other games. Lacrosse balls are easily maintained and may be cleaned with water when necessary. Indoor lacrosse balls are available for indoor practice. The indoor ball is not as lively as the official ball.

Sticks

Lacrosse sticks, often called "crosses," may not exceed four feet in length. Women's sticks usually vary between 3½ to 4 feet in overall length. Length of the player's arms is the prime determinant of the length of stick she will use. The crosse cannot be wider than nine inches at its widest point and cannot exceed twenty ounces in weight. No metal of any kind is permitted on the crosse.

Lacrosse sticks require special attention for proper storage and maintenance. The leather thongs that tighten the gut guard on the left side of the stick should be loosened when the stick is not in use to prevent excess strain on the wood that has been bent to form the angle of the stick. To prevent the handle from warping and the gut from becoming misshapen, sticks should be hung from pegs or hooks, with the wood on the end of the stick resting on the peg or hook. Although there are companies that specialize in the repair of lacrosse sticks, materials may be purchased for repair. Sticks should be wiped dry when wet, sanded if splintering, the wood lightly oiled if dry, and a light coat of petroleum jelly applied to the leather before it becomes brittle and before prolonged storage.

Goalkeeper's Leg Guards, Chest Protector, and Mask

The goalkeeper must be properly protected since the ball often travels through the air

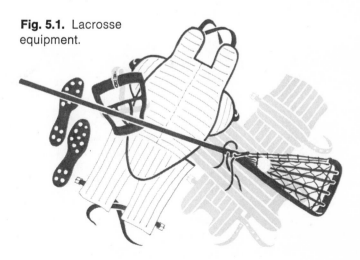

Fig. 5.1. Lacrosse equipment.

on a shot for goal. Leg guards similar to those worn by field hockey goalkeepers protect the lower leg and thigh. Chest protectors that cover the upper thigh, the entire trunk, and around the shoulders are essential. Softball chest protectors do *not* provide sufficient protection and should *never* be used in place of a lacrosse chest protector. Most goalkeepers wear masks, and they are essential for beginning play. *Lacrosse* masks should be purchased, as softball masks usually permit a lacrosse ball to pass between the bars or heavy wire. Goalkeeper's equipment should be kept clean, stored neatly, and scrubbed with a brush and soap and water when dirty. Leg guards may be polished white.

Uniforms

Clothing that permits complete freedom of movement is essential. Many players prefer a kilt and blouse, but shorts or other sports-wear is appropriate if it permits bending, stretching, and running with no restriction. Cleated footwear is recommended since the game is played on grass. Hockey shoes or leather shoes with rubber or composition cleats are appropriate. If cleated shoes are an impractical purchase for instructional classes, beginners may wear tennis shoes but will lose some agility provided by cleated shoes.

Field and Markings

A lacrosse field is a grassy area with goals 90 to 110 yards apart and a minimum width of 50 yards. There are no definite boundary lines. Natural boundaries (e.g., trees, bushes, bleachers) are used to determine out-of-bounds. A center circle with a radius of 10 yards is drawn midway between the two goals. A circle with an 8½-foot radius surrounds each goal cage and is called the goal crease.

Fig. 5.2. Field and markings

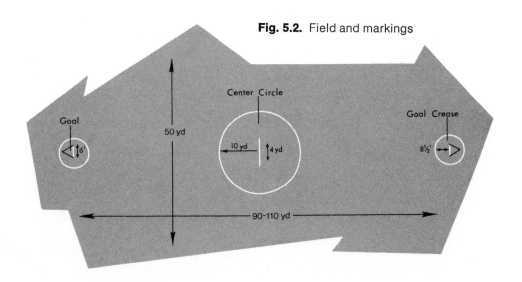

Goal Cages

The goal cage is a six-foot by six-foot square constructed with two square posts and a crossbar. It is recommended that the posts and crossbar be made of wood and painted

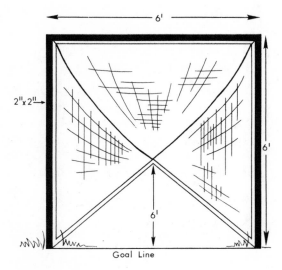

Fig. 5.3. Goal cage

white. Goals made of pipe are legal but are not recommended since rounded surfaces do not produce a "true" rebound. A net is attached to the posts and crossbar and secured to the ground six feet behind the center of the goal line. The net should not permit the ball to pass through.

UNDERLYING SKILL REQUIREMENTS

Lacrosse requires catching and throwing a small ball with a stick and the ability to run quickly and continuously over a period of time. Speed of running is a definite asset as is the ability to change direction quickly

and, for some positions, the ability to run backward. Strength should not be a primary factor except in a long-distance throw. As in all ball games, the player must be able to judge the flight and speed of an aerial and a ground ball. Endurance and conditioning are essential as there is no substitution except for injury, and each half is twenty-five minutes long. Substitution may be permitted in school or college competition. Players must be able to perceive spaces and the movement of players over a relatively large area.

SKILLS

Beginning, intermediate, and selected advanced skills are included in this section. The skills are presented in a teaching progression rather than grouped by function. The beginning skills are those necessary to play a beginning game. The intermediate and advanced skills permit the player to cope with a wider variety of situations. The beginning skills remain basic to the game at any level.

Beginning Skills

Basic skills necessary to play a beginning game are grip, cradle, catch, throw, and pickup off the ground. While dodging, tackling, marking, and other skills are a vital part of the game, they are not required, and beginners will find the few basic skills challenging enough for the beginning game.

GRIP

The crosse, or stick, is gripped with two hands. The top hand is the one usually used in performing an overarm throw in softball or other similar overarm patterns. The *V*

Grip   Grip   Carry

Fig. 5.4. Grip

formed between the thumb and fingers of the top hand is placed at the top of the handle, the collar, just below the last string. With the open face of the head of the stick facing the player, the top hand grips the stick with the palm facing away, the *V* of the hand in line with the *V* of the stick (formed by the wood and gut extending upwards). The top hand grip is diagonal, as in a badminton grip, rather than a fist directly around the stick as in a softball batting grip. The bottom hand grips the handle approximately one-half inch from the bottom of the stick. The *V* of the hand is also in line with the *V* of the stick. The bottom hand grips with a fist directly around the handle as in the softball batting grip.

The grip will seem awkward to many beginners. The top hand grip demands some wrist flexibility which may not be present in some players. The grip is most easily explained with the stick in a vertical position directly in front of the player. It may also be presented with the head of the stick on the ground, open face away from the ground, and the end of the handle or butt leaning against the player. From this position, the player grips with the bottom hand and lifts the stick to an upright position and grips with the top hand.

While gripping the stick with both hands, the player relaxes the arms and lowers the stick from the vertical position for the "carry" position while running. This position should be comfortable and allow the player to run normally.

Beginners should check their grip often until they can assume the correct grip without looking at the stick.

CRADLE

The cradle is the basic skill of the game. Its primary function is to keep the ball in the player's stick with centrifugal force generated by the cradling action while the player is running. But the function of the cradle does not stop there. The cradle keeps the ball loose in the stick so the player may pass accurately; it provides a means of controlling the ball and maintaining possession of it while catching; it provides a means of

Fig. 5.5. Cradle

Cradle to left   Cradle midway   Cradle to right

returning the stick to the upright position without losing the ball on the pickup; and it allows the player to protect the ball and stick with her body against an opponent while on the run. Without the cradle, it is difficult for a player to run with the ball, pick up the ball, catch the ball, throw the ball, and dodge an opponent—all primary and necessary elements of the game.

The cradle is a *controlled* swinging action. The stick is held approximately twenty to thirty degrees from the vertical toward the top hand side. The bottom hand is at least waist height, and preferably closer to chest height, and relatively close to the body. The top arm is extended in an easy, comfortable position, keeping the head of the crosse close to the head of the player, and the forearm parallel to the stick. As the stick is moved to the top hand side, the top wrist rotates outward, and the bottom wrist wraps inward to one side of the body. At this point, the face of the stick is pointing away from the player. The stick then moves with a rhythmical swing to the opposite side of the body. The top wrist wraps the stick around close to the head. The bottom wrist rotates outward with the forearm approximately parallel with or at an upward angle to the ground. The bottom elbow remains in front of the body, and the forearm and wrist pivot around it. The cradling action is timed to the speed of the run. With *each* step the stick is cradled to the side of that step. Therefore, the faster the run, the faster, and necessarily smaller, the cradle.

PROGRESSION AND TEACHING SUGGESTIONS

The most common errors in cradling are:

1. Holding the arms rigid.
2. Allowing the bottom hand to drop below waist level.
3. Failing to keep the bottom elbow in front of the body, resulting in a "sawing" action of the elbow.
4. Swinging the top hand in a wide arc rather than keeping the head of the stick close to the head of the player.
5. Failing to cradle with each step.
6. Running unnaturally or leaping with each cradle.

Cradling is a unique skill. There are no other sports skills with which it may be compared. In a normal running action the arms move forward and back. In the cradling action they move from side to side across the body with little forward and back action. Players must learn to run with a different arm action. For this reason, it is suggested that players learn the cradle at a run, not at a walk. They will have to go through the movements of the cradle slowly, even in a stationary position, in the *very* beginning. But thereafter they should move to a moderate run as soon as possible. After players are running normally, they can go back to various stationary or slow-moving practice to perfect the cradle. Since the cradle is basic to many other skills, players having difficulty with the cradle may also have difficulty with other skills. But players are anxious to catch, throw, and play, and prolonged practice on the cradle at the beginning of a unit can dampen enthusiasm. Since the cradle is involved in other skills, continued practice of the cradle will occur as other skills are practiced. Therefore, new skills should be presented even though all players may not have succeeded with the cradle.

DRILLS

1. Spread over a small area of the field, players cradle in place. Moving quickly

through the group, the instructor checks the basic movements.

2. In twos, without a ball, one player runs and cradles forward ten to fifteen yards and back. Her partner observes and makes comments. After several trials, add a ball to the stick.

3. Several stationary practices can serve as a check for common errors. Players standing with their back against a wall or fence while cradling will find it difficult to "saw" with their bottom elbow as it will contact the wall or fence. Players seated cross-legged, Indian style, are forced to cradle with their bottom hand waist height or above. These types of practice provide a good opportunity for the instructor to check each cradle, make corrections, and provide a rest break from the running drills.

CATCH

Since the ball travels in the air, a player may have to catch the ball at any point or angle within the reach of her stick. The ball is allowed to enter the stick and is kept there with an immediate and continuous cradling action.

In every catch the stick is extended to a position where the player would like the ball to be thrown. From this position she then adjusts to the actual flight of the ball. As the ball approaches, the player angles

Fig. 5.6. Catch

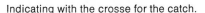
Indicating with the crosse for the catch.   Receiving the ball   The immediate cradle after the catch.

the head of the stick toward the ball, if possible, permitting the ball to run down the face of the stick rather than hit straight on and bounce out. If the ball is traveling fast, the stick gives in the direction the ball is traveling before the cradle. If the ball is lightly tossed, no give is necessary. The first cradle is across the body and is begun as soon as the ball contacts the webbed gut of the stick or immediately after the "give" with a high velocity ball. This first cradle is firm and more definite than subsequent cradles. The stick is "wrapped" around the ball *after* it has entered the stick.

Balls approaching from the player's bottom hand side seem to be the easiest for beginners to catch. The top arm extends quite naturally for the catch. When the ball approaches from the top hand side, the back of the top hand faces the ball. Balls approaching from straight ahead require that the player determine whether they should be caught with the open face of the stick pointing left or right.

PROGRESSION AND TEACHING SUGGESTIONS

The most common errors in catching are:

1. Failing to extend the stick before the catch, resulting in batting at the ball on the catch.
2. Cradling before the catch, resulting in batting at the ball.
3. Presenting a flat surface of the stick toward the ball rather than at an angle.
4. Holding the stick low with the open face pointing upward for the ball to fall into the stick.

Trying to catch the ball can be a frustrating experience for beginners. As a result, some will try any means that seem to be successful. The problem is that some

means that are successful with lightly tossed balls or in a controlled situation may be relatively worthless in different situations. Players should attempt to catch the ball at the first possible moment. This is accomplished by reaching for the ball rather than waiting for it to drop or get too close to the body. Players must experience the ball entering the stick before they can develop the timing of the subsequent cradle. While some balls can be "snatched" from the air with a cradle by more advanced players, beginners attempting this will usually bat the ball away.

DRILLS

1. In twos, one player with a ball, the other player moves at a trot in a small circle around the first player. The ball is thrown ahead of the moving player with a light underhand toss. The ball is returned on the ground to the player in the center. The direction of the run is switched after each five tosses.
2. In short lines, one player with several balls is ahead and to one side of each line. The ball is tossed to the player as she runs forward. The toss can be thrown directly toward the oncoming player and from either side at varying angles.

OVERARM THROW

The overarm throw is used as the basic pass and shot in the game. While the pattern is similar to other overarm patterns, there are differences that can cause negative rather than positive transfer. In preparation for the pass, the stick is cradled to the top hand side with a slightly larger cradle, enabling the top hand to be brought behind and alongside the head. As the stick is brought to this position, the top hand grip shifts slightly to a position with the palm under the stick. The bottom hand remains down, keeping the stick in a general vertical position. The pass is initiated with a lift of the bottom hand, pointing the butt end of the stick in the direction of the pass. In the case of a pass to the top hand side, this will involve an upper body twist in that direction. The top arm extends up and forward and the bottom hand pulls the stick along the throwing arm. The amount of upward thrust and wrist snap of the top hand and the amount of pull of the bottom hand are determined by the length and type of pass.

Fig. 5.7. Overarm throw

| Pulling stick to side of throw | Preparing to throw | After release on the throw |

The top hand action in the pass is similar to throwing a high fly ball in softball.

PROGRESSION AND TEACHING SUGGESTIONS

The most common errors in the overarm throw are:

1. Losing the ball on the take-back of the stick.
2. Pushing the top hand forward rather than throwing.

Losing the ball before the throw is usually a result of a wide, sweeping take-back of the stick. The preceding cradle is larger in that the top arm is taken back behind the usual line of the cradle. If the bottom hand is lifted too high or if it is lifted and not followed by the pass, the ball may roll out of the back of the stick. Pushing with the top hand is probably the most common error of beginners. It can be a result of an incorrect general overarm pattern. The player who has difficulty with an overarm throw in softball, overhand serve in volleyball, or other similar skills, will probably have difficulty with the overarm throw in lacrosse. On the other hand, pushing the ball may be a result of being very careful not to drop the ball and only being required to pass over short distances. While throwing for distance is not necessary in all positions, it is virtually impossible to push the ball over any great distance. Throwing for distance encourages the correct pattern, and beginners should have the opportunity to practice this. Pushing the ball causes it to leave the center of the stick, while throwing the ball causes it to run up the face of the stick and out the tip or end. Players can observe this on their own throws and on the throws of others.

DRILLS

1. In twos, throw and catch over ten to fifteen yards. This should move quickly to a run and cradle with a throw to a moving partner. Each set of players should have enough space to allow the player without the ball to cut in any direction.
2. In twos, spread forty to fifty yards apart or as far as necessary, throw for distance.
3. In groups of five, players are numbered one through five. Player one starts with the ball and passes to player two; player two passes to player three, and so on, until the ball reaches player five, who then passes to player one, and the series begins again. Each group will need a sufficient area so that all players are well spaced. When a player gains possession of the ball, she must run toward the next player who cuts in any direction while calling out her number. Players should not begin their cut until the passer has the ball and is able to pass. The cut should be at top speed in a definite direction. Competition between groups can be organized by counting the number of completed passes or number of consecutive completed passes within a time limit.

PICKUP

The necessity for a method for picking up a ball on the ground will be very evident to beginners. In the process of learning to cradle, catch, and throw, the ball will be on the ground quite often.

The ball may be on the ground in a stationary position or rolling toward or away from a player at various angles. It must be recognized that while picking up a stationary ball is used for beginning practice, the ball is rarely stationary in the game.

Although there are various ways the ball can be picked up, the objective should be to execute the pickup as quickly as possible while on the move to beat and avoid opponents. Slowing down or stopping to pick up the ball invites an opponent to get there first or tackle the player on the pickup. With a stationary ball or a ball rolling away from the player, the object is to move the stick to a low position in order to get under the ball while running at top speed. As the player approaches the ball, the stick is on the side of the bottom hand, with arms toward the ground. As the opposite foot reaches the ball, the knees bend, permitting the player to slide the stick under the ball in a horizontal position. As soon as the ball enters the stick, the bottom hand pushes down toward the ground, bringing the head of the stick up. At the same time, the player begins to cradle to keep the ball in the stick. With as few cradles as possible, the stick is brought to the normal cradling position. The player should attempt to increase her running speed as she picks up the ball and cradles.

When the ball is rolling toward the player, the stick cannot be held in a horizontal position. Instead, the head of the stick is low, almost touching the ground, and the butt of the stick is up so the stick forms an angle with the ground. The faster the roll of the ball, the higher the butt is held, or the greater the angle of the stick with the ground. With a slow-rolling ball, there will be little impact, and therefore no give is necessary to absorb the impact. With a moderate- or fast-rolling ball, the stick must give backward to absorb the impact as the ball enters. Immediately after the ball

enters the stick or as the stick gives backward, the cradle must begin. In as few cradles as possible, the stick returns to the normal cradling position. The pickup occurs as the player runs to meet the ball, and continues running forward on the cradle.

PROGRESSION AND TEACHING SUGGESTIONS

The most common errors in picking up the ball are:

1. Failing to bring the stick to the side of the bottom hand, thereby creating the possibility that the butt end of the stick may be jammed into the player should the head of the crosse stick in the ground.

2. Failing to catch a ball rolling away before attempting the pickup, resulting in pushing or flipping the ball away.

3. Not bending the knees to lower the body and stick on the stationary or ball-rolling-away pickup, resulting in flipping the ball away.

4. Not cradling immediately, resulting in the ball flying or dropping out of the stick.

5. Slowing down while executing the pickup.

The pickup may be introduced before the catch and throw, or players can experiment, up to this point, with picking up the ball without touching it with their hands or body. It is recommended that a few suggestions for picking up the ball be given when players begin cradling the ball and formal presentation of the skill be made after the catch and throw. Players are most anxious to throw and catch and may lack motivation

a

b

c

f

g

Fig. 5.8. Pickup

d

e

a. Preparing for pickup of stationary ball or ball moving away. Front view.

b. Preparing for pickup of stationary ball or ball moving away. Side view.

c. Pushing down with bottom hand on pickup.

d. Cradling up after pickup.

e. Back to normal position after pickup.

f. Preparing for pickup of ball moving toward player.

g. Ball enters stick for pickup

h. Give-back on pickup of ball moving toward player.

to learn the pickup before the throw and catch.

Until the actual game situation, players often do not understand the need for picking up on the run and accelerating as they do so. It is recommended that practices require the players to run while picking up, since picking up the ball while standing still does not require the same timing.

1. Each player has a ball, or players form short lines. The ball is placed five yards away from the player. She runs forward, picks up the stationary ball, cradles a few yards, turns and replaces the ball for her next turn, or the next player.
2. In twos, one player rolls the ball for the player attempting the pickup. This can be used for rolling the ball toward the player and at various angles toward and away.

FIRST GAME SITUATION

Since the position names and positioning on the field are unlike any other sport, it is recommended that the first game situation not include the specific positions of lacrosse. The sport that most closely resembles lacrosse in terms of strategy is basketball. Using some of the features of basketball that may be familiar to some or all of the players can make the first game situation more understandable for them. Teams of ten or more players are divided into offense and defense. Each defense player is paired with an offense player on the opposing team and instructed to mark or guard her as in a player-to-player defense in basketball. Offense and defense can be separated by an imaginary line across the center of

the field as in the old DGWS basketball rules, or several players may act as "roving" players. The age of the players and their familiarity with the game should determine whether artificial separations or boundaries between offense and defense are necessary. A few rules modifications are recommended. Play can begin with a free pass by an offense player from within the center circle. Passing should be the primary means of moving the ball up and down the field to insure the greatest number of players participating. Players can be limited to running only ten yards with the ball before passing. No cross checking should be allowed. The only means the defense can employ to gain possession of the ball are to block the way of an opponent who has the ball without touching her, to intercept passes, and to attempt to pick up dropped or free balls. Each team attempts to move the ball down the field and throw the ball into the opponent's goal. After each goal, the opposing team is given a free pass from the center circle.

Once players have experienced a modified game situation, they should progress to the game itself. The first game situation should indicate the need for further development of beginning skills and the introduction of intermediate skills.

Intermediate Skills

Intermediate skills are not necessarily required by the rules, but they allow the players to cope with a greater variety of situations.

PIVOT TURN

Players often must receive a pass or pick up a ball when they are moving in a course opposite from their intended direction, or away from goal. Therefore, players should be able to turn as quickly as possible and continue in the other direction. The pivot turn is used by players in possession of the ball who wish to change direction.

The turn is executed as soon as the catch or pickup is controlled. The player can turn to either side depending on which foot is forward. If the right foot is forward, the turn will be made to the left; if the left foot is forward, the turn will be made to the right. In preparation for the turn, the forward foot is planted firmly and the stick is cradled to the same side with a firm pull. The weight is over the forward foot. The forward foot pushes off, shifting the weight to the rear foot as the player pivots on both feet. On the pivot, the stick is taken over the head in a cradling action. As the pivot is completed, the player immediately runs and cradles in the new direction.

Fig. 5.9. Turn

Preparatory pull before pivot turn.

Pulling stick over head in pivot turn.

PROGRESSION AND TEACHING SUGGESTIONS

The most common errors in the pivot turn are:

1. Failing to use the pivot turn, resulting in a circular run that is slow and easy to mark.
2. Preferring a turn to one side over the other, causing an adjustment in stride to get the same foot forward each time.

3. Pulling the stick in a wide sweep rather than over and close to the head, usually resulting in a dropped ball.
4. Failing to begin running or cradling, or both, immediately after the pivot, resulting in a dropped ball.

Some players are reluctant to use the pivot turn before their cradling skills are reliable. Although players lacking cradling skills will tend to drop the ball in the pivot

Fig. 5.10. Body checking

Preparing to body check

Following stick while moving with player

turn, they should be encouraged to develop both skills. Once the habit of circling is established, it is difficult to break. The pivot turn allows the player to change direction quickly and efficiently.

DRILLS

Practice of the pivot turn can be combined with simple cradling drills or in combina-

Running with player

tion with several other skills, for example, pickup—cradle—turn—pass.

BODY CHECKING

Body checking does not involve body contact. It is the term used when a player places herself between an opponent with the ball and her goal. The purposes of body checking are to slow the player down, force her off her intended path, force her to pass, and be in position to tackle or crosse check. As the player with the ball approaches the body checker, the latter extends her stick toward the player and prepares to move backwards. When the attacker is approximately five yards away, the body checker begins to move backward to match the speed of the oncoming player. The attacker must slow down, veer away, or pass unless she attempts to dodge the body checker. If any of the first three occurs, the body check has been successful. If the player attempts to dodge, the body checker follows the opponent's stick with her stick and rotates her hips to the side of the dodge so she can run *with* the opponent, always on the goal side. It is important that the hips be rotated, since a player running backward cannot run as fast as a player running forward. Later, when crosse checking is permitted, the body checker attempts to check the opponent's stick as soon as she is within reach and throughout the dodge.

PROGRESSION AND TEACHING SUGGESTIONS

The most common errors in body checking are:

1. Failing to extend the stick toward the opponent, thus making it easier for the opponent to dodge.

2. Failing to start moving backward and being "caught" in a stationary position, making it easier for the opponent to dodge.
3. Failing to rotate the hips in the direction of the dodge.

Body checking requires that the player take small, quick steps in order to change direction quickly. The body checker should realize that she may be successful even if she does not gain possession of the ball.

DRILLS

Drills and practice in body checking are best combined with dodging. Therefore, drills for body checking appear after dodging.

DODGE

A dodge is the means by which a player with the ball eludes an opponent who is between her and goal. The dodger should proceed in her intended direction, directly at the body checker. When she is within five yards of her opponent, she accelerates and, pulling her stick away from her opponent, attempts to pass her. Preceding the pull of the stick for the dodge, the player may feint a pull to the opposite side to deceive her opponent. As the stick is pulled to one side on the dodge, the cradle is continued on that side with a smaller action than in the normal full cradle. The dodger attempts to force the body checker to commit herself to one side and then pulls and dodges on the other side. If the body checker commits her weight on her forward foot—the foot closest to the dodger—in one direction, she can easily be passed on the opposite side. This is referred to as "wrong footing" an

opponent. If the dodger finds that her dodge is unsuccessful in one direction, she may change and pull to the opposite side. In any case, the dodger attempts to remain on a direct line to the goal.

PROGRESSION AND TEACHING SUGGESTIONS

The most common errors in dodging are:

1. Slowing down before the dodge.
2. Attempting to circle around an opponent rather than running directly at her and dodging.

Fig. 5.11. Pulling stick away from opponent in preparation for the dodge.

3. Failing to protect her stick from her opponent by pulling well to the side and continuing to cradle.
4. Failing to accelerate during the dodge.

Players attempting to dodge must understand the objective of the body checker. If the dodger slows down or veers off to one side away from a direct line to goal, she has assisted the body checker. Dodgers must also be aware that to protect the stick from an opponent requires a twist of the shoulders well to the side.

DRILLS

Drills combining dodging and body checking are included in this section.

1. In twos, facing each other without sticks, players grasp the upper arms of their partner. One player is designated as offense (dodger) the other as defense (body checker). As the dodger moves forward, the body checker must move backward. The dodger attempts movements to the right and left; the body checker follows these movements.
2. In twos, facing each other approximately fifteen yards apart, one player with the ball attempts to dodge the other.
3. Dodging and body checking can be combined with various other skills, for example, pickup—turn—dodge—pass.

DRAW

The draw is used to begin each half and after each goal. The *two opposing centers stand with their crosse between the ball and the goal they are defending.** If both

---

* Italics indicate rules which determine how skills are performed.

players grip the stick with the right hand at the top, then both will be facing the goal they are attacking. A left-hand-up player will have her back toward the goal she is attacking. *Both players must have one foot toeing the center line.* The sticks are held about hip level, parallel to the center line. The backs of the sticks are together with wood against wood. The ball is placed between the sticks. *On the signal "Ready . . . draw," the players immediately draw their crosses up and away from one another.* Players attempt to put the ball in the air in the direction of their respective left attack wings. Players should toe the line with their right foot as this allows movement in the direction of the ball. On the signal "draw," each player rasps her stick against her opponent's with an upward movement in the direction of her left attack wing. The top hand must be firm, with the shoulder in line with the hand. As the two sticks lose contact with each other, the player who has moved the quickest with a firm top hand will be able to direct the ball. It is illegal to begin the draw before the signal or to push the ball other than in an up and outward movement. It is quite possible that both players can draw equally, sending the ball straight up in the air.

PROGRESSION AND TEACHING SUGGESTIONS

The most common errors on the draw are:

1. Holding the sticks too high rather than at waist or hip level.
2. Not drawing with a firm top hand.
3. Pushing into the opponent's stick rather than drawing up and out.

The rules no longer require that players draw in the event of a double foul or an

Set for draw

Directing the ball

Fig. 5.12. Draw

injury when no foul was involved. There-fore, all players will not be called upon to draw during the game. Although the two centers are the only players who will draw during the game, all players should experience the skill since they may play a variety of positions.

DRILLS

In groups of three or more, two players draw on the command of the third. Other players are positioned ten yards away, as on the center draw, and attempt to catch the ball.

GOALKEEPING

The goalkeeper wears a mask, chest and body protector, and leg guards. She should

position in front of the goal line within the crease so as to be between the shooter and the goal. She moves with short, quick side steps in a small semicircle in front of the goal line. If the shooter is approaching the middle of the goal, the goalkeeper will be positioned at the apex of the semicircle in front of the center of the goal. Her stick is held in both hands slightly in front on the right side. She must be ready to move in any direction and move the stick to catch the ball at any point or angle. The goal-keeper tries to position her body behind the catch to prevent the ball from going into the goal should she miss the catch or deflect the ball. As soon as the goalkeeper secures the ball in her stick, she should clear the ball to one of her teammates. This may involve a long pass to an attack wing downfield.

Completion or follow-through

PROGRESSION AND TEACHING SUGGESTIONS

The most common errors in goalkeeping are:

1. Positioning back too close to the goal line.
2. Catching the ball off to the side rather than in front of the body.
3. Using the body or hand when a stick catch is possible.
4. Holding the ball too long before clearing.

Beginning goalkeepers against beginning shooters will have a difficult time determining where the ball is likely to be shot. Beginning shooters tend to be inaccurate and do not always attempt the "logical" shot. As players become more experienced and skillful, shots will become more predictable, although the goalkeeper is always at a disadvantage against a close unmarked shooter.

Before players play the position of goalkeeper in the game, they should have some basic instruction and experience. Just putting on the mask, body protector, and leg guards, and attempting to catch and throw, is an experience. As a result of understanding the goalkeeper's position, players will see that shooting, at this level, is nothing more than accurate passing—putting the ball in a space where the goalkeeper cannot stop it.

DRILLS

1. In twos, using tennis balls, one player acts as goalkeeper, the other as a shooter. The shooter throws the ball by hand so that it bounces in front of the goalkeeper. The goalkeeper tries to catch the ball in front of her with her legs together and returns the ball to the shooter. The ball may be thrown at a variety of heights and angles.
2. Players not participating in the game can utilize an extra goal or fence to practice goalkeeping in full pads.

UNDERARM PASS

The ball can be thrown with an underarm action as a pass or shot for goal. It is not as accurate or direct as the overarm pass but does allow the player to easily pass to her top hand side.

The underarm throw begins with a cradle to the bottom hand side of the player. The head of the stick makes a circular arc around, down, and out in the direction of the pass. As the head of the stick drops, the bottom hand raises the butt of the stick

Fig. 5.13. Underarm throw

until the stick is in a vertical position with
the head toward the ground. At this point,
the top hand pulls the stick in the direction
of the pass. The circular action must be
continuous or the ball will drop to the
ground.

PROGRESSION AND TEACHING SUGGESTIONS

The most common errors in the underarm
throw are:

1. Failing to make a circular action with the
   head of the stick, resulting in a push or
   "shoveling" action.

2. Hesitating at some point in the arc,
   allowing the ball to drop to the ground.
3. Pulling with the top hand before the
   stick is vertical, resulting in a throw
   directly to the ground.

The underarm pass can be a valuable
skill, but it is not a substitute for the overarm pass. Players should be discouraged
from throwing underarm when an overarm
pass is possible. Players must understand
and believe that the ball will remain in the
stick if the action is continuous. Otherwise, they will not attempt the circular action.

Drills indicated for the overarm pass, including a throw for distance, may be used for the underarm pass. It may also be practiced as a shot for goal.

CROSSE CHECKING

Crosse checking is an attempt to dislodge the ball from an opponent's stick with a controlled hit or a series of taps with the stick. *The crosse checker may not reach over the shoulder or head of her opponent, touch her opponent, or endanger her opponent with her crosse.* For control of the crosse, both hands are on the stick, and the top hand provides the force necessary for the controlled hit or series of taps. Players may crosse check at any time when an opponent has the ball in her stick, provided it is not dangerous, such as checking the stick upward into the face of the opponent. When body checking, the player extends her stick toward the opponent and follows the movements of her opponent's stick with her own. She then attempts to crosse check without reaching over the shoulder or head of her opponent. Players may also be checked from behind, particularly as they are about to pass.

PROGRESSION AND TEACHING SUGGESTIONS

The most common errors in crosse checking are:

1. Slipping the top hand down and swinging the crosse.

Fig. 5.14. Crosse checking

2. Holding an opponent's stick rather than using a series of taps.

Once players can control the cradle and maintain possession of the ball, it becomes difficult for the defense to secure the ball. Crosse checking should not be introduced while the majority of players are still having difficulty with cradling, catching, and throwing. It can be a frustrating experience to have an opponent hit the ball out of the stick when the player has little success keeping control of the ball on her own.

Players should first attempt to check with a downward tap on the stick. Later, as players become more skillful and controlled, they can use upward taps as well.

DRILLS

1. In twos, facing each other approximately fifteen yards apart, one player with the ball attempts to dodge; the other attempts to body check and crosse check.
2. Various situations which incorporate crosse checking with other skills can be designed. For example, in drills involving passing, catching, and picking up the ball, an opponent can be added to body check and crosse check.

SHOOTING

Shooting is, basically, accurate passing. The basic shots for goal are the long bounce shot, close overarm shot, and close underarm shot.

The long bounce shot is effective when the shooter is fifteen to twenty yards away from the goal. The ball is directed out and down with a hard overarm pass action so

that it bounces just inside the crease, in front of the goalkeeper, and rebounds into the goal.

The close overarm shot is not a hard-thrown ball. This shot is placement of the ball into a space not covered by the goalkeeper. If a player with the ball moves across in front of the goal, she forces the goalkeeper to move. As the goalkeeper moves, an overarm shot directed back to the original position of the goalkeeper is often effective.

The underarm shot is often used when the player with the ball moves across in front of the goal with her top hand side closest to the goal. While an overarm shot can be executed with a twist of the upper body, an underarm shot may also be performed. This shot is directed at an open space or back as the player moves in front of the goal.

PROGRESSION AND TEACHING SUGGESTIONS

The most common errors in shooting are:

1. Throwing the ball in the direction of the goal rather than planning a controlled, well-placed shot.
2. Shooting at the goalkeeper rather than at spaces.
3. Shooting through other players on the field.

In beginning games, players will tend to become excited and their skills erratic. Shots at goal, under these conditions, are often throws in the direction of the goal with the hope that somehow a goal will be scored. As players develop their skills and understanding of strategy, shots for goal should become planned and controlled.

1. In short lines, approximately twenty yards away from the goal, players, in turn, throw the ball into the air, run forward to catch the ball, and shoot a long bounce shot. Various angles to the goal should be utilized.

2. Close shots may be practiced at all angles, particularly moving across in front of goal. In short lines off to one side of the goal, players run across in front of goal until they are past the midpoint of the goal at which point they shoot to the back corner, using an overarm or underarm shot.

3. One set of five to ten players form a semicircle approximately fifteen yards from the goal with an opponent between them and goal. In turn, each outside player with a ball runs directly toward goal to shoot. Her partner will body and crosse check while the player attempts to shoot. After each set of players have had a turn, the outside players rotate one position to the left and inside players rotate one position to the right so all have new opponents.

Selected Advanced Skills

While there are a number of skills in lacrosse that can be classified as advanced, most advanced skills are refinements of the basic skills. Advanced players are able to catch the ball at all angles within their reach, pass the ball accurately long and short, and in general, perform basic skills at a high level. Practices at this level should require the players to execute skills in as many different situations as possible.

SIDEARM PASS

The sidearm pass is useful as a short pass when a player is marked by an opponent. The stick is lowered to a horizontal position with the top hand about waist level. The ball is thrown and directed primarily with the top hand.

SHOOTING

Advanced players can develop different shots for different situations. A shot similar to the 'round the head shot in badminton can be used when the shooter is almost past the goal with her top hand side away from goal. This shot is directed to the upper corners of the goal with a soft placement. The underarm shot may be directed high or low into the goal or may roll on the ground. It may also be used to propel the ball with a strong lever action directly into the goal.

STRATEGY

The team in possession of the ball is on offense; the team without the ball is on defense. Lacrosse requires the direct interaction of teams on the field. Each team consists of twelve players.

The official game consists of two twenty-five-minute halves with no time-outs except for injury. Substitution may be made only in the event of an injury or if modified rules permit substitution at half time or at the discretion of the umpire. Each goal counts as one point. Each team attempts to score as many goals as possible and to prevent the opposing team from scoring. It is toward these respective ends that lacrosse strategy is aimed.

Basic strategy remains basic to all levels of play.

Offensive Strategy

The game begins with a center draw. Players line up for the center draw as shown in figure 5.15. As soon as the draw is completed, one team will gain possession of the ball and be on the offense. At this point basic patterns of offense develop. Offensive patterns are used to create spaces into which players may cut to receive the ball and to provide some means of replacing the player who has cut. Figure 5.16 shows two different basic offensive patterns. The first and third homes tend to pull to the same side to create spaces in the middle of the

Fig. 5.15. Lineup for center draw

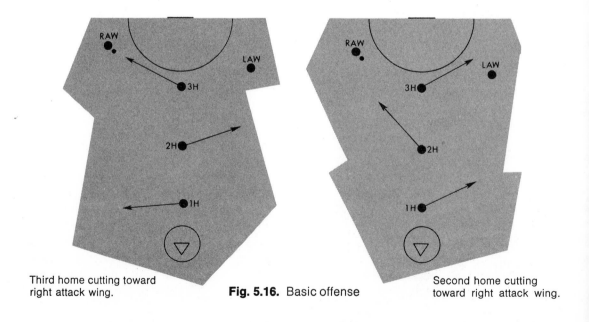

Third home cutting toward right attack wing.

Fig. 5.16. Basic offense

Second home cutting toward right attack wing.

field. The second home pulls in the opposite direction. The third home cuts toward the player with the ball when it is up field. As the player with the ball is level with the third home, the second home cuts to receive the pass. Ideally, two or three players are cutting in various directions on each pass. Obviously, all three cannot receive the pass. Players who cut and do not receive the pass must quickly reevaluate the situation and position for another cut. Players will often receive a pass when moving away from goal. These players are called "connectors" as they connect to help advance the ball down the field. Players who cut toward the goal, and often away from the player with the ball, are called "cutters" as they will be in position to shoot after the catch. Beginning players should generally be discouraged from cutting away from the player with the ball, as they will often be blocked from a pass by their opponent, and the player with the ball has difficulty passing when everyone is running away from her. Players should be encouraged to pull away from where they want to catch the ball so as to create a space into which they may then cut.

In general, the attack wings play on the sides of the field, receiving the ball from the defense and feeding it to the homes. They may cut into the center of the field to receive a pass and go for goal but should not continuously remain in the center of the field. When an attack wing cuts to the center, one of the other attack players should *replace* her on the wing. The center acts as a link between the defense and the offense in the center of the field. She will have opportunities to move toward the goal and shoot but should not remain close to goal. Again, when the center moves toward goal, one of the other attack players should re-

place her at center. The center and the attack wings tend to move vertically up and down the field. The homes tend to move horizontally at various angles.

While the attack can pass, catch, and shoot even when their opponents are marking, offensive strategy attempts to get a free player advancing with the ball. Once a free player with the ball is moving toward goal, it forces the defense to interchange and be one player short, leaving one attack player free. Attack players must understand the defense interchange in order to take advantage of the free player situation. The free attack player with the ball should run directly toward goal, and if no defense shifts to tackle her, she should shoot. If a defense player does shift to tackle her, she must know who the free player is as a result of the shift. The player whose opponent goes to tackle the free player should first pull away to make it difficult for her opponent to shift. Then as her opponent leaves her, she should cut, toward goal if possible, to receive the pass. The second home will find herself in this position most often, since her opponent, the cover point, usually is called upon to shift onto the free player.

Different positions require some different kinds of abilities. The following briefly outlines these abilities for each attack position.

FIRST HOME

The first home is positioned closer to goal than any other attack player. She must be able to control the ball in small spaces with opponents close by. She should have a variety of very reliable short shots. The first home should be able to run in short spurts over relatively short distances.

SECOND HOME

The second home must be ready to replace the first home, the third home, or either attack wing when necessary. She must be able to take advantage of the defense interchange. She should have a variety of reliable moderate and short shots. The second home must have a quick burst of speed over short to moderate distances.

THIRD HOME

The third home must make the decision whether to cut toward the player coming downfield with the ball or to pull away. She often determines the movement of the other homes. She should be able to run quickly over moderate to longer distances. She should possess good long and moderate shots. The third home may replace the center, attack wings, or second home.

ATTACK WINGS

The attack wings should have good, sustained speed over relatively long distances. They should possess good long and short shots.

CENTER

The center must be able to run from goal to goal throughout the game. Her position is both attack and defense. She should possess good speed over long periods of time. She should possess good long and moderate shots.

GENERAL OFFENSIVE STRATEGY

1. Each player with the ball should have two or three options as to teammates to whom she may pass, unless she is shooting.
2. Players must cut and recut, always repositioning while the ball is at their end of the field.
3. The objective of the offense is to score a goal.
4. Free attack players in front of goal have a great advantage over the goalkeeper.

Defensive Strategy

Defensive strategy begins with the lineup for the center draw. Each defense player is between her opponent and goal and, in the case of the third man, cover point and point, with her opponent on her top hand side. This begins the *player-to-player marking* or guarding system. The defense begins directly next to her opponent. As the ball moves up and down the field each defense player continues to mark her opponent closely. The objective is to mark her opponent so closely that the ball cannot be passed to her. If the ball is passed to her opponent, the defense player's first consideration is whether or not she can intercept the pass. If the possibility is realistic, she attempts the *interception*. If she cannot intercept, she positions to attempt to *crosse check* immediately as the ball enters her opponent's stick. If this is not possible, she positions between her opponent and goal, ready to *body check*. Therefore, the defense player must make an immediate judgment based on the position of the ball, her opponent's position, her position, her opponent's speed, and her speed. This judgment must be made as the ball is passed. Should an attack player get free of her defense, the remaining defense must be ready to pick up this free player. The system by which a free attack player is covered is called *defense interchange*.

If the free attack is in an attack wing position, the cover point will interchange to check the free player. The cover point waits until she can move directly into the path of the free attack between the attack and goal. Until this point, she marks her second home. The defense wing on the opposite side of the field from the free attack moves in and marks the second home. The other attack wing is left free, as she is the least dangerous attack player at this point. The defense player who was initially lost or beaten by her opponent moves quickly toward goal and picks up the free player resulting from the interchange. Should the second home be the free attack,

the point must shift at the last possible moment to prevent a free shot at the goal. The closest defense wing will shift to the first home. If the free attack is the center, and the third man is in position to interchange, she should do so. The closest defense wing would then shift to the third home if the third home is in position to participate in the play. Otherwise, the defense wing would remain with her attack wing, while continuing to watch the movements of the third home.

Once a defense player gains possession of the ball, the entire team goes on offense. Defense players leave their opponents to cut and assist in moving the ball down the field to the attack players. The ball is usually moved to the side if it is close to goal.

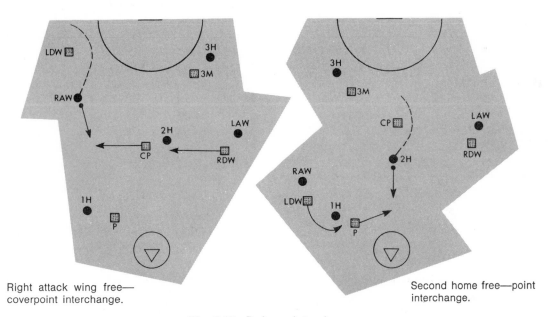

Right attack wing free—coverpoint interchange.

Second home free—point interchange.

Fig. 5.17. Defense interchange

Defense wings and third man may enter the attack with the ball as a free player to initiate an attacking move. This should not be done continuously, as an interception or loss of the ball will leave an opponent unmarked.

If the goalkeeper gains possession of the ball, she can clear to a cutting defense nearby or make a long clear downfield to an attack wing.

Different positions may require some different abilities. The following briefly outlines some of these differences by specific position.

POINT

The point marks the first home almost exclusively. She must be able to move in small spaces and cover one of the best shooters on the opposing team. She should be able to pick up a ball and quickly move out of a congested area. She should be particularly skilled at body checking and crosse checking.

COVER POINT

The cover point tends to be the pivot of the defense. She must be able to make judgments and move quickly in the defense interchange. She marks the second home, often the best shooter on the opponent's team. She must be particularly skilled at body checking and crosse checking and possess good speed over moderate distances.

THIRD MAN

The third man marks the third home. She must have good speed over moderate distances. She should be ready to initiate the attack as a free player.

DEFENSE WINGS

The defense wings mark the opposing attack wings. They must be ever alert for the defense interchange. They should have good speed and be aware that they can initiate the attack as a free player.

CENTER

The center marks the opposing center and is also considered a member of the attack. She must be able to mark her opponent all the way to the goal line, yet be in position to link the defense and attack and participate in the attack.

GOALKEEPER

The goalkeeper should be able to catch the ball from every conceivable angle. She must possess a certain courage to refrain from ducking or shying away from the ball. She must be agile, quick moving, and must react quickly. She should have the capability for throwing the ball accurately over a long distance.

GENERAL DEFENSIVE STRATEGY

1. Once a judgment has been made, the player should move quickly and definitely.
2. A defense player's objective is that her opponent will not touch the ball.
3. Players must switch quickly from defense to offense.

BASIC UNIT PLAN FOR BEGINNERS

The following eighteen-lesson unit plan is designed as a guide for instruction. Each teaching situation will be unique. Players should play the game as soon as possible. Strategy and rules are best presented as situations occur; however, time is allotted for these items in this plan. It is assumed that appropriate warm-up activities will precede each lesson. These should relate to the game and the skills as much as possible. Each instructor should select review items based on student need. After the first game situation, some time should be devoted to playing the game in each lesson where possible.

Lesson 1   Grip—cradle
Lesson 2   Cradle—catch
Lesson 3   Overarm throw—pickup
Lesson 4   First game situation
Lesson 5   Turn—draw—game
Lesson 6   Dodge—body checking
Lesson 7   Game
Lesson 8   Passing—game

Lesson 9   Offensive strategy
Lesson 10   Defensive strategy
Lesson 11   Game
Lesson 12   Shooting—crosse checking
Lesson 13   Review rules—game
Lesson 14   Game
Lesson 15–18 Tournament play

SELECTED BIBLIOGRAPHY

DGWS. *Field Hockey-Lacrosse Guide.* Washington, D.C.: AAHPER. Published every two years.

BOYD, MARGARET. *Lacrosse, Playing and Coaching.* Rev. ed. London: Nicholas Kay Ltd., 1971.

DELANO, ANNE LEE. *Lacrosse for Girls and Women.* Dubuque, Ia: Wm. C. Brown Co. Publishers, 1970.

LEWIS, B. J. *Play Lacrosse the Easy Way.* London: Candium Press, 1970.

Soccer, Speedball, and Speed-a-Way

Soccer is a universal team sport, usually called football in countries other than the United States. It is played competitively by men throughout the world. Women have adopted most of the elements of the men's game, but soccer is rarely played in organized competition by women. It is played in instructional classes and intramural programs.

Speedball is an American game created in 1921 for men's intramural play. Since that time, the rules have been adapted and played almost exclusively by girls and women. It is primarily an instructional class and intramural sport with interscholastic competition in some areas of the country.

Speed-a-way rules were first published in 1950. It resembles speedball, but its rules are more lenient and it permits running with the ball as in American football.

Official rules for women's soccer and speedball are published in a combined *Guide* every two years by the Division for Girls and Women's Sports of the American Association for Health, Physical Education, and Recreation. Official speed-a-way rules are published by the Burgess Publishing Company.*

* 426 South Sixth Street, Minneapolis, Minnesota.

EQUIPMENT

Balls

An official soccer ball may be used for soccer, speedball, and speed-a-way. Official balls are leather-covered and twenty-seven to twenty-eight inches in circumference. While leather balls are official, they are more expensive than rubber-covered balls. The expense of the leather ball and the durability of the rubber ball must be weighed against the points that the leather ball is easier to handle, both with the feet and hands, and does not "sting" on contact. Older leather balls tend to absorb moisture and become sodden.

Although an official soccer ball is permitted in speed-a-way, the rules recommend the use of an official speed-a-way ball. This ball is of a different size and surface than a soccer ball and permits a higher bounce.

Wet balls should be wiped dry after use. Storage areas should not be excessively hot or dry.

Uniforms

Shorts and shirts or other types of clothing designed for activity are appropriate for soccer, speedball, and speed-a-way. Rubber-cleated shoes with extra protection on the inside of the instep and over the toes are recommended. Smooth-soled canvas or leather shoes may be worn for beginning instruction. Shin guards may be worn for protection.

Field, Markings, and Goals

SOCCER AND SPEEDBALL

The official playing field is eighty to one hundred yards long and forty to sixty yards wide. It should be a level, well-trimmed, grassy area. The soccer goals are six yards wide and eight feet high. For speedball, the goal posts should extend to a height of twenty feet.

SPEED-A-WAY

The official playing field is one hundred yards long and sixty yards wide with a recommended minimum of seventy-five yards long and forty-five yards wide. The goals are four yards wide and seven feet high as in women's field hockey. The rules do permit the substitution of soccer or speedball goals, football goal posts, field hockey goals, or temporary goals of benches or towels to make the game adaptable to many situations.

UNDERLYING SKILL REQUIREMENTS

All three sports require kicking and running. Speedball and speed-a-way require the handling and throwing of the ball by all

Fig. 6.1. Soccer, speedball, and speed-a-way fields and markings

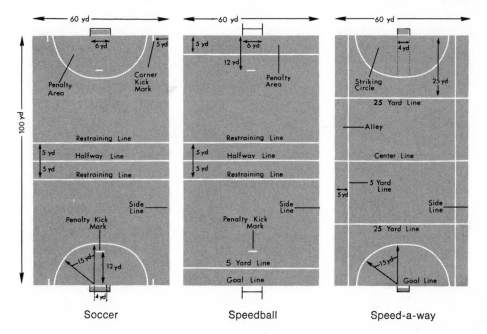

Soccer   Speedball   Speed-a-way

players, and speed-a-way permits running with the ball. The major prerequisites are speed and agility in running. A certain amount of strength is necessary for kicking a long ball and, when permitted, throwing the ball over a distance. The ability to change direction quickly and control the ball with quick movements of the feet is necessary, as speed and accuracy are required by the games. Since there is direct interaction of the teams, each player must be able to perceive and move about in small and large spaces with other players moving at the same time.

SKILLS

This section contains beginning, intermediate, and selected advanced skills of soccer, speedball, and speed-a-way. The soccer skills are presented first, and the reader is referred back to these skills for speedball and speed-a-way. Only the skills unique to speedball and speed-a-way and, therefore, different from soccer skills are presented in the speedball and speed-a-way sections.

The beginning skills are basic to the game and those necessary to play a beginning game. Intermediate and advanced skills, though important to the game, are not absolutely necessary for beginning official play.

Each skill is described in terms of its use, analyzed, and followed by common errors of learners and suggestions for teaching the skill. Drills follow each skill or group of skills. Practice in gamelike situations is stressed.

Soccer Beginning Skills

The skills necessary to play the game are basic trap of the ball on the ground, dribble,

and short kick or pass. Although there are a number of traps and volleys for receiving and controlling the ball, they are not all necessary for a beginning game. Kicking the ball over long distances may be required for good strategy and in shooting for a goal, but a short pass or kick will suffice in the beginning and does not require exceptional fielding skills.

SIDE OF THE FOOT TRAP

The ability to field, intercept, or change the direction of the ball is basic to the game. The side of the foot trap is the most basic and the easiest means to control a moving ball. The purpose of any trap is to receive the ball in such a way as to be able to dribble, pass, or kick immediately.

As the ball approaches from any angle, the player gets in line with the ball and decides whether to trap the ball with the inside or outside of the left or right foot. The trapping foot is raised a few inches off the ground and turned out if trapping on the inside or turned in if trapping on the outside of the foot. The ball is allowed to rebound *slightly* as the body moves with the ball in the direction the player wishes to go.

PROGRESSION AND TEACHING SUGGESTIONS

The most common errors of beginners in trapping the ball with the side of the foot are:

1. Kicking at the ball rather than "gathering" it in.
2. Waiting on one foot ready to trap rather than going to meet the ball.
3. Allowing the ball to rebound a distance away rather than judging the speed of

the ball and "giving" with the impact when necessary.

As this skill may be the first introduction to the soccer ball, a hand-rolled ball may be used for practice. It is important that the learner experience successful performance quickly so as not to discourage further attempts. The learner should then experience the "feel" of the ball and handling the ball with the feet in a variety of situations.

DRILLS

Players should be moving to trap the ball as soon as possible. The speed of the ball should be slow to begin, increasing as the practice continues.

1. In partners or small groups, one player rolls the ball to another to trap.
2. In lines, one player rolls the ball diagonally ahead for the player running forward to trap.
3. In shuttle formation, one player rolls the ball for the oncoming player to trap.

DRIBBLE

The dribble is a means of advancing the ball while maintaining possession. The ball is advanced by a series of short taps with the feet so as to keep the ball close to the feet of the running dribbler and away from any opponents. It is used when an opponent is not close and there are no players on the

Fig. 6.2. Dribble

same team who are in a more advantageous position than the dribbler. A pass travels more quickly than a dribble, and players should be coached to pass rather than dribble whenever possible. Dribbling can easily become an overused skill. It also serves as a means to control the ball after a trap or interception and when maneuvering to set up a play.

The basic dribble uses the inside of the feet. The ball is kept within a few strides of the dribbler by rotating the leg outward and pushing or tapping the ball forward with alternate feet. It is not necessary to contact the ball on each stride; however, the ball should not be more than one or two strides away from the dribbler. The ball will have a forward and slightly diagonal path with each tap. Players should be encouraged to run with as normal a stride as possible, with the tapping foot slightly off the ground at contact and the body forward with the head over the ball.

PROGRESSION AND TEACHING SUGGESTIONS

The most common errors of beginners in dribbling are:

1. Kicking the ball and sending it too far ahead where it can easily be intercepted.
2. Not running with a normal stride and hopping on one foot in order to contact the ball.
3. Watching only the ball and not being aware of teammates and opponents.
4. Being overly deliberate and careful, resulting in covering very little distance at a slow rate.
5. Overusing the dribble when a pass would be more effective.

Control is essential in the dribble, but speed is also necessary. In presenting the

dribble, *both* elements should be stressed. The players will need to be reminded to look up between dribbles.

DRILLS

After getting the "feel" of dribbling, players should practice as close to game speed as possible.

1. In lines, one player from each line dribbles forward twenty yards and back.
2. If a relay is used to increase speed, players must contact the ball a predetermined number of times, for example, two contacts every five yards, otherwise players will kick and run rather than dribble.
3. In twos, small groups, or lines, one player rolls the ball to another who fields the ball on the run, dribbles to a spot, and then rolls the ball for the next player.

INSIDE OF THE FOOT KICK OR PASS

This kick is useful as a short pass and for shooting a goal. It is a natural outgrowth of the dribble and, therefore, is a natural teaching progression after the dribble has been presented. The kick is controlled and is effective over short distances. The ball is in position as for the dribble. The kicking leg, with foot rotated outward, is drawn back and swings forward from the hip with the knee slightly flexed. The leg straightens after the foot contacts the ball. The right foot is used for a kick to the left; the left foot is used for a kick to the right. The ball can be kicked straight ahead with either foot by rotating the kicking leg sharply out before the swing of the leg forward. In each case, the ankle is stabilized on contact, and

Fig. 6.3. Inside of the foot pass

the foot contacts the ball midway between the toes and the heel.

PROGRESSION AND TEACHING SUGGESTIONS

The most common errors made by beginners performing the inside of the foot kick are:

1. Trying to kick the ball when it is too far away, resulting in a weak kick or no kick at all.

2. Trying to kick the ball when it is too close, resulting in a weak kick or tripping up the player.
3. Succumbing to the natural instinct to kick the ball with the toe.

Kicking the ball with the inside of the foot is not a natural action, and many beginners are tempted to kick the ball off the end of the toes. While it is possible to kick the ball in this way, it can be painful if the kicker's shoes do not have reinforced toes and can be a most inaccurate pass. To encourage the use of the inside of the foot pass, keep the distance of the passes short and emphasize that it be done on the run.

DRILLS

Kicking from a stationary position does not prepare the player for passing while running. While there are times in the game when a pass is executed from a stationary position, the emphasis should be on passing a moving ball while on the run. When passing from a dribble, emphasize a quick pass, using as few dribbles as possible to control the ball.

1. In twos or small groups, one player dribbles once or twice and passes to another who receives, dribbles, and passes.
2. In partners, players move half the length of the field, dribbling twice and passing to each other.
3. Five lines of players simulate the forward line, the first person in each line operating as a group. The ball starts with the right wing. Players are instructed to pass the ball to the player on their left as they move quickly down the field. On the next turn, the ball starts with the left wing and the procedure is reversed.

4. Using the same formation as in drill number 3, alternate the starting position of the ball with the five positions, instructing the players to pass the ball, without taking more than two dribbles, to any other player and to end with a shot into the goal.

FIRST GAME SITUATIONS

Since soccer requires the direct interaction of two teams, it is easier to begin game play with reduced-size teams on smaller than regulation fields. Six-player teams can play on one half of the field. The field of play utilizes the sidelines of the official field as goal lines. Pinnies or towels can mark the goals. The halfway line and goal lines of the official field act as the sidelines for the six-player game. Four teams of six players each can play and be supervised at one time on one official-size field. Teams are divided into three offense and three defense—centers, left, and right. Defense players are to mark one opposing offensive player. Four extra players may be added as goalkeepers to keep the defense from drifting off their players to protect the goal.

Play starts with a free kick by one of the offense players midway between the end lines. With only six players on a team, it is easier to keep the players separated and to begin basic offensive and defensive strategy. Only necessary rules are needed, keeping the game as simple as possible, for example, a free kick for the opponents for touching the ball with the hands; a throw-in by the opponents for balls kicked over the sidelines; a defense kick or corner kick for balls sent over the end lines. Elaborate strategy need not be developed at this point. After players have experienced this modified form of play, they are ready to try the game with regulation-size teams on a regulation field. The instructions should be kept to a minimum, stressing passing rather than dribbling and each defense player marking the appropriate offense player. Further strategy and rules should be introduced as the situations occur.

Soccer Intermediate Skills

The skills in this section are considered intermediate because they are not absolutely necessary to play the game. They are, however, a vital part of the game and permit the players to deal with a greater variety of situations.

INSTEP KICK

The instep kick can be used for a moderate to long pass or shot for goal with a stationary or moving ball. Whether or not the ball is moving, the player usually approaches the kick with a run. The nonkicking foot is placed to the side of, or slightly behind, the ball for support. The kicking leg is extended backward, with the knee flexed to a ninety-degree angle. As the leg swings forward from the hip, the knee extends and the toes are pointed down. The ball is contacted slightly below midpoint by the top of the instep or the lacing of the shoe. The force of the swing and the point of contact will determine the trajectory and velocity of the ball.

PROGRESSION AND TEACHING SUGGESTIONS

The most common errors by beginners when performing the instep kick are:

1. Kicking with the toe rather than with the top of the instep.

2. Contacting the ball above the midline, sending the ball along the ground.

3. Contacting the ball too low and sending it high and not deep.

4. Attempting to kick a ball that has not been controlled, resulting in a miss or an inaccurate kick.

Many beginners erroneously believe that the instep kick should be kicked with the end of the toes and will attempt to prove it. Through demonstration and experimentation, they should discover the value of the true instep kick. Players should be encour-

aged to control a moving ball before attempting to kick it and not just swing their leg at any ball near them. With the possibility of a number of players being within a small area, several players flailing their legs and feet at the ball is not only inefficient and leads to inaccurate passes, but can cause injury.

DRILLS

1. In twos or small groups, players fifteen yards apart kick stationary balls to each other.

Fig. 6.4. Instep kick

2. In twos or small groups, players dribble three to five yards and kick a moving ball to each other.

3. In threes or small groups, one player dribbles and kicks to another who traps the ball, dribbles for control, and kicks to another player. Players should be well spaced to encourage longer kicks.

4. The passing drill utilizing five players in position as a forward line can be repeated, using both long and short passes.

PUNT

The punt is used only by *the goalkeeper*, as she *is the only player permitted to touch the ball with her hands while in the field of play*.* It is a strong kick that travels over the heads of players. It is used by the goalkeeper to clear the ball away from goal and start the attack of her own team.

The ball is held in two hands about waist height in front of the body. A step with the nonkicking foot is taken in the direction of the punt. As the kicking leg, with knee bent, swings forward from the hip, the ball is dropped so as to contact the instep of the kicking foot as the knee extends. The closer to the ground contact is made, the lower the

* Italics indicate rules that determine how skills may be performed.

Fig. 6.5. Punt

flight of the ball, and conversely, the farther from the ground contact is made, the higher the trajectory of the ball.

PROGRESSION AND TEACHING SUGGESTIONS

The most common errors in punting are:

1. Throwing the ball up in the air before contact.
2. Throwing the ball toward the ground before contact.
3. Not watching the ball or mistiming the kick so that contact is made with the shin or toes.

Although punting is a skill used only by the goalkeeper in soccer, all players should be familiar with the punt since beginners are usually given the opportunity to experience all positions on the team. The concept of *dropping* the ball is difficult for beginners. The natural tendency is to throw the ball up and out for the kick. This makes punting with any accuracy very difficult and should be discouraged from the beginning. It is not advisable to practice punting for too long a period at any one time since beginners may bruise their lower legs with miskicks.

DRILLS

1. Partners, facing each other over twenty to thirty yards, take one or two steps and punt to each other.
2. One player passes the ball to another who picks it up, bounces it once, and immediately punts to another player downfield.

SOLE OF THE FOOT TRAP

The sole of the foot trap is relatively simple to perform but becomes more difficult as the player runs faster. It is a means of controlling a relatively slow-moving ground ball. As the ball approaches, the player extends one leg toward the ball, with the foot off the ground at approximately a forty-five-degree angle. The ball is allowed to roll into the space between the sole of the foot and the ground and is trapped.

Fig. 6.6. Sole of the foot trap

ONE- AND TWO-LEG TRAPS

The one- and two-leg traps are used primarily by beginners on ground balls that approach the player from straight ahead. They are slow but sure traps and make it difficult to play the ball immediately because the player must first recover from the trap. On the one-leg trap, the player must be in line with the oncoming ball. As the ball approaches, the player is in a forward stride position, with weight forward over a bent knee. As the ball enters the space between the knee and ground, the knee is flexed with weight still forward, trapping the ball. The two-leg trap is similar to the

Fig. 6.8. Two-leg trap

one-leg trap but the feet are parallel. As the ball reaches the player, both knees are flexed, and the ball is trapped by both legs.

INSIDE OF THE THIGH TRAP

The inside of the thigh trap is used with low-bouncing balls or balls in low flight off the ground. As the ball approaches, the player turns the inside of the thigh of the trapping leg toward the ball, with the knee bent. The height of this leg is determined by the height of the ball. The ball is allowed to contact the inside of the thigh between the knee and the hip. On contact, the leg

Fig. 6.7. One-leg trap

Fig. 6.9. Inside of thigh trap

Fig. 6.10. Chest trap

should "give" back, allowing the ball to drop to the ground near the feet.

CHEST TRAP

The chest trap is used when the ball is in the air at chest height. Girls and women find this trap awkward since they must protect their chest with their arms. As the ball approaches, the player folds her arms across her chest. In order *to contact the ball with any part of the arm or hand, these parts should remain in contact with the body.* The player leans forward from the waist and "gives" back on contact.

PROGRESSION AND TEACHING SUGGESTIONS

The most common errors in trapping are:

1. Allowing the ball to rebound away from the body.
2. Having difficulty in judging the flight of the ball and determining which trap is appropriate.
3. Moving the arms away from the body in the chest trap.

All traps are called traps because the player should be in direct control of the ball following contact. This is not the case if the ball is allowed to rebound any distance away from the player. Therefore, the player must judge the flight and speed of the ball, select the appropriate trap, and "give" when necessary to cause the ball to drop near her feet.

DRILLS

It is suggested that a thrown ball be used for practicing trapping in the beginning. Kicked balls can be very inaccurate at this level, players may have difficulty in lofting the ball, and some trappers may be frightened by a hard kick until they have practiced the skill. Later, kicked balls should be used so that the players are ready to handle what will occur in the game.

1. In twos or small groups, players roll and throw the ball to each other for trapping.
2. In small circles, one player in the middle of the circle throws the ball to any player in the circle to trap the ball. Each trapper should attempt to finish with the ball near her feet.

Fig. 6.11. Knee volley

VOLLEYS

Volleying the ball is allowing the ball to rebound off some part of the body to a teammate. This makes a volley unlike a trap, although some traps may be used as volleys. Basic volleys are done with the knee, hip, shoulder, and head. Volleying with the head, or *heading*, is described in the section on selected advanced skills. In the knee volley, the knee is bent and is pointed toward the lofted ball. The ball is contacted on the upper portion of the knee, permitting the ball to travel through the air to a teammate. In the hip volley, the hip is turned toward the ball with a forward movement to contact the ball. In the shoulder volley, the arms are usually folded across the chest for protection in the event that the ball is missed with the shoulder and strikes the chest. The player turns the shoulder toward the oncoming ball and contacts the ball with

Fig. 6.12. Hip volley

the upper portion of the arm near the shoulder. *The arm should remain in contact with the body.*

PROGRESSION AND TEACHING SUGGESTIONS

The most common errors in volleying the ball are:

1. Allowing the ball to volley indiscriminately rather than directing it toward a teammate.

2. Misjudging the ball and missing the volley.
3. Not contacting the ball squarely and losing accuracy.

Not all girls and women are comfortable volleying a hard-kicked ball and may duck away or close their eyes. Practice should begin with lightly tossed balls to build confidence. Until players have developed confidence, they should not be forced to contact hard-kicked balls. If players in the game situation or in practice seem to be avoiding contact with the ball, this is a good indication that they do not have confidence in their skills and may be afraid of the ball.

DRILLS

The same drills used for trapping can be used for the practice of volleying. The player attempts to volley the ball back to the thrower or kicker or to another player.

THROW-IN

The throw-in is used primarily by side halfbacks to put the ball in play after it has gone out-of-bounds over the sideline. It is the only skill in which the ball is legally handled by players other than the goalkeeper. The rules are very permissive regarding the throw-in. *The player may throw the ball with any type of one- or two-hand throw.* For a two-hand throw, the ball is held overhead and thrown as in the two-hand overhead pass in basketball, resulting in a relatively short pass. A one-hand throw permits a longer pass and can be thrown like an overarm throw in softball or as a sidearm sling much the same as throwing a discus.

Fig. 6.13. Two-hand throw-in

PROGRESSION AND TEACHING SUGGESTIONS

This skill should present little difficulty. As a carry-over or transfer from other activities, students should be able to throw the ball in some way. The concentration in this unit should be on throwing long and short passes to free teammates in such a way that the receiving player is able to control the ball.

DRILLS

1. In partners or small groups, players throw long and short passes to each other, the receiver trapping or volleying the ball.
2. In a small modified game situation, each player has the opportunity to throw in the ball from the sideline to teammates who are marked by opponents and spaced on the field.

DODGE AND TACKLE

Generally, players should be encouraged to dribble only when not closely marked and pass whenever possible. There will be occasions, however, when the player with the ball must attempt to evade (dodge) an opponent who is trying to take the ball away (tackle). Dodging is a continuation of dribbling and protecting the ball with the body. There are no rules prohibiting the player from obstructing an opponent or shielding the ball with her body. Dodging involves faking a pass and dribbling on with the ball; faking dribbling to one side of an opponent and going to the other side; swerving when approaching an opponent; and changing the pace of the dribble. In changing the pace of the dribble, the player with the ball slows down and permits the tackler to advance. She then speeds up quickly and attempts to pass the oncoming tackler.

Tackling is the attempt by one player to gain possession of a ball being dribbled or controlled by another player. The tackler has been successful if she forces the dribbler to give a poor pass, if she deflects the ball, if she causes the dribbler to slow down, or if she gains possession of the ball. As the dribbler approaches, the tackler should watch the movements of the dribbler and

Fig. 6.14. Side or hook tackle

not be misled by deceptive movements. The tackler should time her tackle when the ball is off the dribbler's foot. There are two basic tackles: the straight tackle and the side, or hook, tackle. In the straight tackle, the tackler either traps the ball with the sole of her foot or with one or two legs. In the side, or hook, tackle, the tackler is to one side of the dribbler. She extends the leg closest to the ball and, in effect, traps the ball with her foot and lower leg. In both cases, the ball is then pulled toward the tackler and away from the dribbler.

PROGRESSION AND TEACHING SUGGESTIONS

The most common errors in dodging and tackling are:

1. Dribbler failing to be aware of the tackler and dribbling directly into the tackler.
2. Dribbling too loosely, making a tackle easy.
3. Attempting to force the ball past an opponent, involving body contact.
4. Tackler kicking at the ball rather than trapping.
5. Tackler tackling the player rather than the ball.

Dodging and tackling should not be a mutual flailing of legs but rather a skillful attempt to elude or trap. Players should be discouraged from blindly kicking in the general direction of the ball.

DRILLS

1. In twos, one player attempts to dodge, the other to tackle, at normal running speed.

2. In modified game situations involving three- to six-player teams, each team attempts to reach an objective, that is, a boundary line or goal, by passing, dodging, and tackling.

Soccer Selected Advanced Skills

The following skills may not be taught in the basic instructional program. They represent the skills of the more advanced player or competitor. Progressions, teaching suggestions, and drills are presented only for the skills that are unlike those presented in previous sections.

OUTSIDE OF THE FOOT DRIBBLE

The outside of the foot dribble is used to keep the body between an opponent and the ball and when changing direction of the ball, instead of dribbling with the inside of the foot.

SHORT PASSES

The outside of the foot, the sole of the foot, and the heel may be used for short kicks or passes. The outside of the foot pass is similar to the inside of the foot pass, except that the ball is contacted on the outside of the instep with an outward swing or push of the leg. The sole of the foot and heel kicks are used to propel the ball backward to a teammate. It is difficult to perform these passes with a moving ball. In the sole of the foot pass, the sole of the foot is placed on top and slightly to the front of the ball. The ball is passed backward by flexing the knee and pushing back with the foot. The heel kick is executed by extending the leg backward, contacting the ball in the center with the heel.

VOLLEY KICKS

The volley kick is used when the ball is in the air or after the ball has bounced. The foot position is the same as in the instep kick but the ball is contacted in midair. The half volley kick is similar to the volley kick except that the ball is contacted just after it hits the ground as in the half volley stroke in tennis. The half volley kick is the same as the dropkick except that the ball has not been dropped from the hands.

DROPKICK

The dropkick is used exclusively by the goalkeeper in soccer. Executed correctly, it produces a hard kick with a low trajectory. The ball is held in the hands as for a punt. As a step is taken with the nonkicking foot, the ball is dropped to the ground. The kicking leg swings forward from the hip, the knee extends, and the ball is contacted with the top of the instep or toe *just after* the ball hits the ground. The most difficult part of the dropkick is the timing of the contact. If the ball is contacted too soon, it results in a low and weak punt. If it is contacted too late, it results in a drop *and* kick with a high trajectory. Players should be instructed to analyze their own timing and be able to differentiate between a punt, a drop and kick, and a dropkick.

HEADING

Heading the ball is volleying the ball with the head to a teammate as a pass, bringing a high-lofted ball to the ground, or as a shot for a goal. Not all girls and women are anxious to head the ball; and bobby pins, clips, and other such items should not be worn in the hair when heading. A ball below the waist should not be headed, as the player may be kicked. The player should watch the ball carefully as it approaches in the air. The player jumps to meet the ball in the air, with the center of the ball being contacted at the hairline. The upper body and neck should be well set against the impact, and the arms are out to the side for balance. Players should keep their jaw closed during contact.

Speedball and Speed-a-way Skills

All of the basic skills of soccer are basic to speedball and speed-a-way. The emphasis in the game is different, however. Soccer is a game played with the feet and body, and rarely may the ball be played with the hands. The emphasis in speedball and speed-a-way is to legally convert a ground ball into an aerial ball so that the ball may be played with the hands. Because of the different methods of scoring, speedball and speed-a-way require greater emphasis on the punt and dropkick. Throwing the ball becomes essential, as do skills that enable a player to legally lift a ground ball to herself or teammates and thus convert a ground ball into an aerial ball. The reader is referred to the basketball skills section for catching, throwing, footwork, and guarding skills.

The differences in the rules of speedball and speed-a-way permit slight variations in the methods by which ground balls may be converted into aerial balls. *In speedball, either the foot must leave the ground or the ball must leave the foot or leg before it is touched with the hands. In speed-a-way the ball must be off the ground but may be resting on the feet or legs and picked up in the hands. In speed-a-way a kicked ball may be caught in the hands after it has taken one bounce. This is illegal in speedball.* All conversions legal in speedball are legal in speed-a-way. All conversions legal in speed-a-way are not necessarily legal in speedball.

LIFTS TO SELF

There are several methods by which a ground ball may be converted to an aerial ball by an individual player. With a *stationary ball,* one foot is placed on top of the ball, and with a quick movement, the ball is drawn toward the player with the sole of her foot. As the ball moves, the toe of the same foot is quickly placed under the rolling ball and lifts or flips the ball upward to be caught. In speedball, the foot must leave the ground or the ball must be off the foot before it can be caught. In speed-a-way, the ball may be taken off the foot provided the ball is not touching the ground. In both speedball and speed-a-way, a player can place both feet alongside a stationary ball, squeeze the feet together, and jump with both feet, knees out to the side, lifting the ball into the air. As she jumps, she reaches down to catch the now aerial ball. In speed-a-way *only,* the ball may be squeezed between the feet until it is off the ground and then picked up off the feet.

Fig. 6.15. Lift to self

Fig. 6.16. Lift to self

With a *moving ball*, one leg is extended toward the ball, with the toe pointed toward the ground. As the ball rolls onto the foot, the ball is flipped into the air or the foot is lifted off the ground for the catch and conversion in speedball. In speed-a-way, the ball may be taken off the foot or allowed to run up the leg for the catch. In speed-a-way *only*, the ball may be allowed to roll onto two feet in side

stride position. From this position, the player rocks back onto her heels and picks up the ball.

LIFT TO A TEAMMATE

There is one basic method in speedball and speed-a-way for lifting a ground ball to a teammate to convert to an aerial ball. The toe and instep of the lifting foot are placed

Fig. 6.17. Lift to teammate

or slid under the ball with the weight on the nonlifting leg. The knee of the lifting leg is bent, and the foot is extended. With an extension of the knee, the ball is lifted with the foot and toes into the air to another player. In speedball, the ball must be caught before it hits the ground. In speed-a-way, the ball may be caught after one bounce.

PROGRESSION AND TEACHING SUGGESTIONS

The most common errors in converting a ground ball to an aerial ball are:

1. Attempting lifts to self with opponents too close.
2. Not being aware of the conversion opportunities and playing the ball primarily on the ground.
3. Picking the ball up off the ground in confusion between ground and aerial balls.

Lifts to self tend to be too slow with a stationary ball if there are any opponents near. They should only be used when opponents are far enough away to permit the time necessary to execute the lift. If the students have played soccer, they will have to be reminded about the conversion possibilities, otherwise speedball or speed-a-way games will lack the elements that make them games different from that of soccer.

DRILLS

1. In twos or small groups, players lift to self using different methods.
2. In twos or small groups, one player rolls the ball to another who lifts to self.
3. In twos or small groups, one player lifts to another.

4. In a modified game situation of teams with two to six players each, players start with a ground ball. Each team attempts to convert to an aerial ball against opponents within a specified area. Score one point for each conversion, and the ball is returned to the ground after each conversion.

SOCCER STRATEGY

The team with the ball is on the offense; the team without the ball is on the defense no matter where the ball is on the field. Soccer requires the direct interaction of teams on the field. The game consists of four eight-minute quarters. Each team attempts to put the ball, by legal means, across the goal line and into the opponent's goal as many times as possible. The defensive teams attempt to intercept or gain control of the ball before it can be shot into their goal. It is toward these ends that all strategy is aimed.

The strategy presented in this section is basic to all levels of play. Because of the similarity of the strategy of soccer and field hockey, the reader is referred to the field hockey section on strategy wherever and whenever appropriate.

Offensive Strategy

The game begins with a kickoff in the center of the field. Figure 6.18 shows the positioning of the offensive teams for the kickoff. From this point, the offensive strategy is very similar to that of field hockey, and the reader is referred to the field hockey offensive strategy section. One obvious difference is that the soccer ball can easily be sent over the heads of players for long or

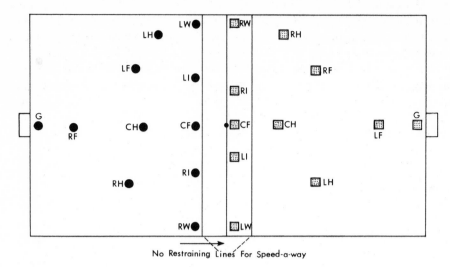

Fig. 6.18. Lineup for kickoff

No Restraining Lines For Speed-a-way

short distances, whereas in field hockey this type of play is not typical. This leads to the two most common types of offense in soccer: the long passing and the short passing attacks. The long passing attack utilizes the ability to pass long distances over the heads of players. The short passing attack more closely resembles that of field hockey.

Specific plays can be developed for the specific situations that occur in the game. These situations include the kickoff, throw-in, and corner kick.

On the *kickoff*, the offensive team has direct possession of the ball. This is unlike the center bully in field hockey in which each team theoretically has an even chance to gain possession. As a result, a specific plan can be employed in the soccer kickoff. The ball is usually kicked to the left or right inner who then may (1) give a short or long leading pass to the closest wing, (2) pass ahead to any other free forward breaking down the field, or (3) pass back to

a halfback who then passes downfield to a forward.

On a *throw-in*, the type of strategy employed will depend upon the positioning of the ball and opponents just as in the roll-in in field hockey. When in the defensive end of the field, the ball should generally be thrown downfield away from the goal area. In midfield, the thrower has all the options of a long or short throw to any free player. Close to goal, the thrower should attempt to set up a shot for goal. In this case, she looks for a free player near the center of the field in position to shoot or a free player in position to pass into the goal area for another player to shoot.

The *corner kick* situation is similar to the corner in field hockey. The defense has sent the ball over their own end line, and the corner kick is taken by an offensive player on the goal line, five yards from the corner. The major difference is that the offensive team may be anywhere on the field rather than being restrained by a striking circle. This difference means a difference in strategy. The corner kicker usually tries to send the ball in the air across the mouth of the goal so that a member of her team can volley the ball into the goal. Generally, the wing should take the kick, varying the height and spin on each kick. The other forwards should move to create spaces into which the ball can be kicked.

GENERAL OFFENSIVE STRATEGY

1. The type of play should be varied to confuse the opponents.
2. The ball should be passed or thrown to the feet of a teammate for control.
3. Players should pass whenever possible rather than dribble.
4. Players should pass ahead to a closely marked player and directly to the player if her defense is not close.
5. A pass across a team's own goal should be avoided unless passing safely to the goalkeeper.
6. Pull away from a teammate with the ball to avoid bunching.

Defensive Strategy

Basic defensive strategy in women's soccer is almost identical to that of field hockey, and the reader is referred to the field hockey defensive strategy section. It is basically a player-to-player defense with provisions for covering free players depending on the position of the ball. Although the strategy of field hockey and soccer at beginning and intermediate levels for women is almost identical, highly competitive play in soccer utilizes zone defense. At the advanced level of play, certain differences demand differ-

ent approaches. Since girls and women do not play highly competitive soccer, the similarities with field hockey are usually stressed for the eventual transfer to the game of field hockey which is played at highly competitive levels by girls and women.

The following information on soccer defensive play is specific to soccer. On the *kickoff*, the defensive team is relatively certain that the offensive team will retain possession on the first pass. Their responsibility at this point is to mark their opponent as quickly as possible, with the forwards on the defensive team attempting the first interception. On the *corner kick*, the defensive team's halfbacks, fullbacks, and goalkeeper must be behind the end line until the ball is kicked. Therefore, the defensive forwards should mark opposing halfbacks and forwards who are pulled back from the goal line. Defensive halfbacks and fullbacks should move quickly on the kick to mark forwards close to the end line. A *defense kick*, resulting after an offensive player has sent the ball out of bounds over the end line, should be taken by a fullback or the goalkeeper. If the goalkeeper takes the defense kick, one of the fullbacks should cover the goal.

Zone defense in soccer requires that the player with the ball be marked by the player in that zone. Zone defense does not attempt to actively mark each offensive player at all times. It is similar in concept to zone defense in basketball. A combination player-to-player and zone defense can be employed. In midfield, the defense players within the area of the ball mark the offensive players in that area. When the ball gets close to goal, all offensive players are marked by an opponent.

The *goalkeeper* in soccer has many of the same responsibilities as the goalkeeper in field hockey. However, there are some differences in the requirements of the position in soccer. The goalkeeper alone may handle the ball within the field of play. She should use this advantage whenever possible. She should be ready to catch rolling, bouncing, or aerial balls in her hands, always placing her body between the ball and the goal. If the ball is too high to catch, she can tip the ball by placing her hand under the ball and cause it to go over the crossbar rather than into the goal. While she should always attempt to gain control of the ball, the goalkeeper may punch or strike the ball to change its direction in an emergency situation. Diving at the ball should be used only as a last resort.

GENERAL DEFENSIVE STRATEGY

1. The entire team is on the defense when the opposing team has the ball. Forwards should tackle back quickly when they lose the ball.
2. Defense should mark players closely and not roam all over the field.
3. More than two players on the ball should be avoided.
4. Defense should clear the ball up the sidelines away from goal.
5. Passing or dribbling across in front of goal is dangerous and should be discouraged.

SPEEDBALL AND
SPEED-A-WAY STRATEGY

The basic concepts of offense and defense in soccer apply to speedball and speed-a-way. The major difference is that the offensive team should attempt to convert a ground ball into an aerial ball whenever possible. In speedball, the highest scoring play is a dropkick over the crossbar. A dropkick can only be attempted from an aerial ball. Similarly, the touchdown in speedball and speed-a-way can only be scored from an aerial ball. The offense should always attempt to score the highest number of points but should be aware of *all* of the possibilities for scoring and not concentrate on only one to the exclusion of the others. It is far better to score from a ground ball than lose the ball in an attempt to score from an aerial ball. The defense must be able to switch quickly from the ground game of soccer to the aerial game which is much like basketball.

BASIC UNIT PLAN FOR BEGINNERS

Soccer

An eighteen-lesson unit plan is presented as a guide for instruction. Warm-up and review are basic to each lesson and should be selected by the instructor to best meet the needs of her situation. It is suggested that warm-up utilize the skills of the game. Rules, strategy, and officiating are best taught as the situations develop in skill learning and game play. However, time is allotted in the plan for these items. It is assumed that time will be devoted to play for some portion of most lessons.

| Lesson 1 | Introduction—inside of the foot trap—dribble—inside of the foot pass |
| Lesson 2 | Modified or six-player teams |

Speedball and Speed-a-way

Since both games require the skills of soccer, the following unit assumes that soccer skills have been covered previously. For this reason, nine lessons are presented that can be used as guides for both speedball and speed-a-way.

SELECTED BIBLIOGRAPHY

DIVISION FOR GIRLS AND WOMEN'S SPORTS. *Soccer-Speedball Flag Football Guide*. Washington, D.C.: AAHPER. Published every two years.

LARSEN, MARJORIE S. *Speed-A-Way*. Rev. ed. Minneapolis: Burgess Publishing Co., 1960.

NELSON, RICHARD L. *Soccer for Men*. 2nd ed. Dubuque, Ia.: Wm. C. Brown Co. Publishers, 1971.

Softball

Softball is a popular team sport played by girls and women throughout the United States. Derived from the "national" sport of baseball, its greatest appeal is as a recreational pastime and in organized league competition. The first official women's rules were adopted by the National Section for Girls and Women's Sports in 1927. Current official rules are published every two years by the Division for Girls and Women's Sports of the American Association for Health, Physical Education, and Recreation.

EQUIPMENT

Gloves

Ideally, each player expected to catch a softball should have a mitt or glove. First baseman's and catcher's mitts are distinguished from fielder's gloves by their shape and construction. Mitts do not have individually separated fingers. The catcher's

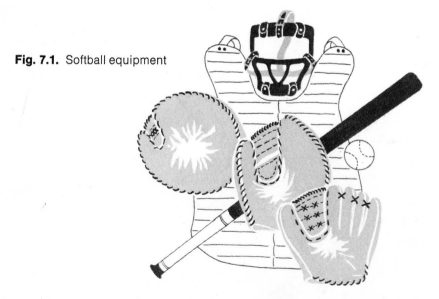

Fig. 7.1. Softball equipment

mitt has a deep pocket surrounded by heavy padding. The first baseman's mitt is less padded and is designed to trap the ball. Increasingly, many catchers are using first baseman's mitts in competition. Fielders' gloves are fingered gloves, usually four or five fingers and a thumb. Inexpensive gloves can be purchased, but those chosen should be constructed of soft leather, with no bunching of padding, and should be stored carefully so that their shape is not altered. All leather should be cleaned periodically and treated with oil at the end of the season to prevent cracking or splitting. Storage areas should not be excessively hot or humid.

Balls

Leather balls are ideal for handling and play, but rubber-covered balls may give longer service for classes. The rubber-covered ball, however, is hard and may not be as appropriate for beginners. Larger "slow pitch" softballs have less velocity on impact and can be used in modified play at the lower age levels. Leather balls absorb moisture and become heavy and misshapen when used in damp or wet weather. Official specifications are given in the DGWS *Guide.*

Bats

A variety of lengths and weights should be available for each age level. Baseball bats should not be used for softball. Weight, length, and size of grip are individual to each player, and each player should have the opportunity to experiment with several different bats. Bats should be kept clean and should be stored to prevent damage to grips or splintering. Rough edges should be sanded, and any bat suspected of being cracked or split should be broken and disposed of to prevent injury. A broken or split bat should never be taped and used. Aluminum bats that are very durable for instructional and competitive play are available.

Uniforms

The usual wear for physical education classes is appropriate for beginning softball. When sliding is permitted and for competitive play, participants should wear long pants for protection of the legs. Ideally, shoes with cleats (hard rubber or metal) should be worn for competition. Smooth-soled canvas or leather shoes will suffice for beginning play.

Masks and Protectors

The catcher and plate umpire must wear face masks and body protectors. The masks should be well padded, the padding covered with smooth leather or other suitable material. The body protectors should fit comfortably, and sizes large enough to fully protect even the larger girl should be furnished. Leg protectors are available for greater protection and for competitive play. Masks and protectors should be hung or stored to prevent marring of the soft leather of the mask or disturbing the distribution of the padding in the body protector.

Field, Markings and Bases

A softball diamond may be set up on a level field area approximately two hundred by two hundred feet. For the safety of the players, the grass area should be well trimmed and smooth. Portable or permanent back-

Fig. 7.2.   Field and markings

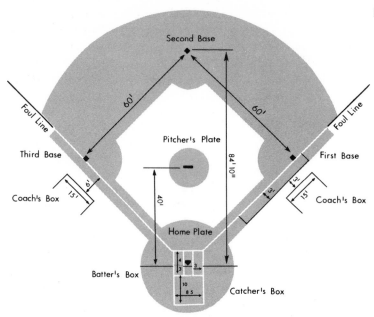

stops should be available for the official game. For instructional classes and competitive play, base lines, batter's box, and catcher's box should be clearly marked. Although small, unpadded "throw" bases are less expensive, they will not remain in place and, therefore, should not be used. Bases should be fastened firmly in place with the metal stake pounded well into the ground. Bases should be taken in each day, brushed, and stored flat. A permanent pitching rubber and home plate should be level with the surrounding field.

UNDERLYING SKILL REQUIREMENTS

Softball is a throwing, catching, batting, and running game. A certain amount of strength is necessary to throw the ball with speed and accuracy. Quick reaction time is a prerequisite for infielders and batters, and

good depth perception is necessary for outfielders and batters. Good base running demands quick starts and sprinting speed. The participant must be psychologically prepared for the speed and impact of a batted or thrown ball so as not to shy away or duck from an oncoming ball. For some girls, this demands a great deal of courage and confidence in their skills.

SKILLS

This section is organized into beginning, intermediate, and advanced skills. The beginning skills are those necessary to play an official game, and they remain basic to the game at any skill level. The intermediate and advanced skills enhance the game and challenge the player. At each level, the skill is described in terms of its use. Each skill is then analyzed, followed by suggestions for progressions for learning and other teaching suggestions. Suggestions for drills for improvement of performance follow each skill or group of similar skills. Emphasis is placed on gamelike practice situations wherever possible.

Beginning Skills

The skills necessary to play a game are catching, fielding (forms of catching), throwing, pitching, and batting. Modified games can be played before all of these skills are well developed.

CATCHING

Catching is basic to the game of softball. Each pitch must be caught by the catcher, unless it is hit by the batter, in which case someone must catch or field the batted ball. A baseman contributes little to the game unless she catches balls that are thrown to her. As a prerequisite to catching, the player should be instructed regarding how to wear a glove or mitt. The glove or mitt is worn on the nonthrowing hand in such a way that the base of the fingers of the hand are approximately in the center of the palm of the glove. Many beginners attempt to place their fingers too far into the fingers of the glove, making it almost impossible to "squeeze" the ball when it enters the glove and also making the impact painful. Beginners should be encouraged, and probably required, to wear gloves for their own safety and confidence.

Catching requires (1) moving the body so as to be behind and in line with the flight of the ball, (2) determining the speed (velocity) of the ball and positioning accordingly, (3) placing the glove properly to intercept the ball, and (4) keeping one's eyes on the ball until it enters the glove. The arms should extend to meet the ball, whenever possible, to allow for the dissipation of

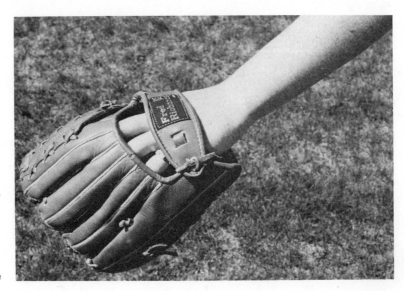

Fig. 7.3. Wearing a glove

energy, but *not* to the point of holding the arms rigid or locking the elbows. As the ball enters the glove, the other hand should be alongside the glove to assist in squeezing the ball to keep it in the glove. The amount of "give" required will depend upon the speed of the ball. There is no "give" when catching a lightly tossed ball.

FIELDING GROUND BALLS

Fielding ground or bouncing balls is simply a low catch. The generalization of keeping the fingers down for a catch below the waist and fingers up for a catch above the waist holds true under most situations. Again the body should be behind and in line with the ball, the speed and trajectory determined, and the eyes watching the ball. The fielder should attempt to move toward the oncoming ball to cut down the number of bounces or amount of field over which it must travel and to decrease the amount of time before a throw can be made. In order to be on line with a low ball, the fielder must bend while moving toward the ball. Ideally, the ball should be caught next to the foot on the same side as the throwing arm while on the move so a throw can be executed quickly after the catch.

FIELDING FLY BALLS

Fielding fly balls is simply a high catch. Determination of the velocity and trajectory is most important for the correct positioning

Fig. 7.4. Fielding a ground ball

for the catch. All other aspects of catching previously mentioned apply to the catching of fly balls. The ball should be caught at approximately eye level, six to eight inches in front of the face.

PROGRESSION AND TEACHING SUGGESTIONS

The most common mistakes of beginners in catching the ball are:

1. Inability to determine the velocity and trajectory of the ball.
2. Hyperextension or locking the elbows in anticipation of the catch.
3. Closing the eyes or turning the head away from the ball just before impact.

4. Failure to use the throwing hand to assist in squeezing the ball in the glove after the impact or squeezing too soon, permitting the ball to rebound off a "closed" glove.

All of these mistakes can usually be corrected by practice and individual instruction. Consideration of the items on the foregoing list may aid in the initial presentation of skills and suggests where emphasis can be placed during instruction.

It is difficult to teach catching without throwing. The teacher cannot throw the ball to each student so that each might practice catching. Therefore, the overarm throw may be presented at the same time, and drills would involve both skills. There is

Fig. 7.5. Fielding a fly ball

some benefit, though, in teaching the three forms of catching at one time because of their obvious similarities. Students can experiment with throwing before actual instruction is given. The experimentation may point out just where the difficulties are in throwing, making the teaching of throwing more meaningful. There will be some inaccuracy in throwing even after instruction.

DRILLS

In all cases, the students should be moving as soon as possible rather than performing in a static position. The drills should also approximate what will be required in the game situation. For example, the fielding of a ground ball should be followed by a direct throw. The following drills assume one ball for each two persons, but the same drills could be used with three or four in a group.

1. Easy direct throws between partners, primarily for warm-up and application of the principles of catching.
2. Partners approximately ten to fifteen yards apart throw high fly balls to each other. After initial throws, partners should throw the ball slightly long, short, left, or right so that the receiver must move. Control must be exercised by the instructor so that deviations do not become excessive yet are challenging. If throwing skills warrant, move the partners farther apart.
3. One partner throws the ball along the ground; the other catches and immediately makes a direct throw back. This approximates that which will be required in a game situation, as fielding a ground ball is never followed by the throwing of another ground ball.

OVERARM THROW

There are many reasons given as to why girls and women seem to have difficulty with the overarm throw. Perhaps the main reasons are lack of proper instruction at the elementary school level and the feeling of many girls that "throwing like a girl" may be more socially acceptable. The overarm throw is basic to the game of softball, just as the overarm pattern is basic to many sports.

The ball is gripped with four fingers and thumb spread on the ball, the thumb in general opposition to the four fingers on top of the ball. The ball should not rest on the base of the fingers or the palm. Some players prefer to grip the ball with two fingers and thumb, but most girls' hands are not large enough to do so and still maintain control. The ball is taken directly back to a position approximately eight inches above shoulder height, the upper arm extended back, wrist cocked back, elbow pointing diagonally toward the ground, and the opposite shoulder pointing in the direction of the throw. The take-back will vary with the position of the catch. The throwing action is initiated with the beginning of the step in the direction of the throw with the foot opposite the throwing arm. The torso then twists in the direction of the throw, followed by the shoulder, elbow, hand, and wrist. Each of the actions is a cue to the next and should be executed in a smooth, continuous action. For this reason, it is difficult to perform any part of the throw without the other parts. Kinesiological cinematographic analysis indicates that the fastest movement in the throw is the inward rotation of the shoulder joint, with the upper arm parallel to the ground, followed by the

Fig. 7.6. Grip for
overarm throw.

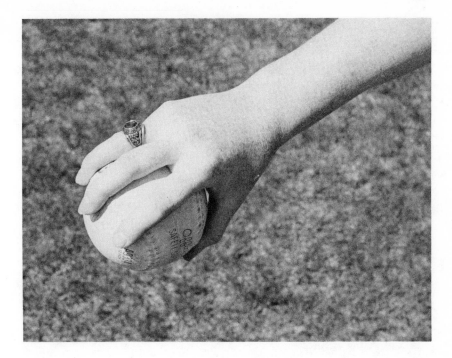

wrist snap forward. It is this action that
gives power and direction to the ball. For
control, the ball leaves the fingertips of the
first three fingers last.

PROGRESSION AND TEACHING SUGGESTIONS

The most common mistakes in the overarm
throw are:

1. Gripping the ball with the palm.
2. Pointing the elbow in the direction of
   the throw in the take-back.
3. Initiating the action with the arm rather
   than the body, often accompanied with a
   step forward on the throwing-side leg.
4. Lack of power due to lack of rotation of
   the shoulder and lack of wrist snap.

Teaching of the overarm throw should
not be taken lightly. For many students,
the first instruction in an overarm pattern
occurs in softball, and improper techniques
at this stage can cause difficulties in other
sports skills requiring an overarm pattern.
Speed as well as accuracy should be emphasized from the beginning in order to develop
the proper technique. It must be remembered that the overarm throw is not a direct
overhead throw. The lower arm action falls
twenty or more degrees from the vertical
plane. When the deviation from the vertical
plane reaches forty-five or more degrees, it
becomes a sidearm action.

Students will perform skills in ways that
bring them success. It is extremely important that practice situations do not allow
improper techniques. Success depends on
correct techniques, for they do not limit
further skill development.

DRILLS

1. Short throws between partners, primarily for warm-up and application of basic principles. Do not concentrate on short, easy throws.
2. Partners, twenty yards apart, throw and catch direct throws.
3. Partners, twenty or more yards apart, throw the ball as high as possible. It is extremely difficult to throw the ball high over a distance with incorrect techniques.
4. With a partner, or against a target on a wall ten to fifteen yards away, throw the ball as hard as possible yet still maintain control.

MODIFIED GAMES   Gamelike situations can be used after basic understandings of catching, fielding, and throwing have been developed.

1. Shuttle relays over ten to fifteen yards using:

   a. Direct throws
   b. Ground balls
   c. Fly balls

   Relays can destroy the skills being practiced. In this case, the relay emphasizes speed and accuracy and should not encourage improper techniques.

2. Game of 500. In groups of six, one player throws ground and fly balls within a specified area. Each ground ball caught and held counts 50 points; each

Fig. 7.7. Overarm throw

fly ball caught and held counts 100 points. First player to score 500 points wins and becomes the thrower. Groups must be kept small to insure participation by all.

3. Using a softball diamond, two teams play a regulation-type game with the "batter" catching an overarm throw from the pitcher, or a toss from the catcher, and bats by throwing the ball into the field. This enables all to successfully "bat" in some manner and can begin instruction in the game itself.

Games such as "Beat the Ball" can be entertaining but can be in opposition to the requirements of the actual game and are, therefore, not recommended.

PITCHING

The underhand, fast-ball pitch is basic to all levels of play. Curves, drops, and spins should be the skills of the advanced pitcher but will not be mastered in an instructional class. A player will be more successful with a good fast-ball pitch than with mediocre skills in a variety of pitches.

Pitching becomes highly specialized and individual; however, all beginners should have the opportunity to learn basic pitching.

The pitcher stands in a forward stride position with the heel of the throwing-arm foot on the front edge of the pitching rubber and the toe of the opposing foot on the back edge of the rubber. The rules indicate that *both feet must be in contact with the* rubber with shoulders squarely facing the plate.* The grip will vary with the size and strength of the hand and the preference of the pitcher. Many girls and women cannot control the ball without all four fingers and the thumb gripping the ball. In this case, the grip is the same as for the overarm throw except that the palm is up. The ball may also be held in a tripod fashion with the first and second fingers and the thumb forming the tripod.

The ball must be held with two hands in front of the pitcher for a minimum of one second and a maximum of twenty seconds. From this position the pitcher cannot move the ball toward the plate without releasing

---

* Italics indicate rules that determine how skills may be performed.

the ball. The ball is brought back in a semi-circular swing down and back, the elbow straightening, the shoulders and hips rotating back with the swing. At the height of the backswing, the arm is fully extended and the wrist cocked back. The forward motion is initiated with a step with the leg opposing the pitching arm. The arm whips forward with an underhand pendulum motion as the hips and shoulders rotate forward. *The pitcher may not take more than one step without simultaneously delivering the ball to the batter. The hand must be below the hip and the wrist may not be farther from the body than the elbow.* The point of release is determined primarily by the speed of the ball; however, *the release must occur beyond the straight line of the body.* The ball leaves the fingertips last as

Fig. 7.8. Grip for fast-ball pitch.

the wrist snaps forward. After the release, the trailing leg should be brought opposite the forward leg so as to be in a balanced fielding position. This pitch is also called the slingshot pitch.

PROGRESSION AND TEACHING SUGGESTIONS

The most common errors in pitching are:

1. Lack of backswing, lack of body twist, or lack of wrist snap, resulting in lack of power.
2. Ball released too early or too late, resulting in a very low or a very high pitch.

The problems of speed and accuracy apply to the pitch as well as to the overarm throw. A slow, looping pitch, although it goes over the plate, is not an effective pitch except as a change of pace. Students should be encouraged to pitch as hard as they can while maintaining some degree of accuracy. Students will not become good, accurate pitchers in several lessons. Practice should be at the regulation distance of forty feet, and as soon as possible with a target. This target can be marked on the wall, strings outlining the strike zone, or a home plate and a catcher.

DRILLS

1. In twos, pitch over a twenty-foot distance for warm-up and application of principles.
2. At regulation distance, pitch a ball to target on a wall, through strings outlining the strike zone, to rebound net, or to a catcher over home plate.

Fig. 7.9. Basic pitch with slingshot delivery

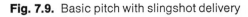

BATTING

Batting is the primary offensive skill in softball. While it is possible to get on base, or even score a run, without hitting the ball, in such a situation the player is hoping for a pitcher error rather than initiating the play herself.

The batter must stand within the batter's box of three feet by seven feet when hitting the ball. For long-ball hitting or "swinging away," the bat is gripped very near the lower end of the grip so as to lengthen the lever arm and increase the velocity of the bat. For a right-handed hitter, the left hand is at the bottom, the right hand next to the left and nearer the top of the bat. Some advocate that the second joints of the top hand be in line with the knuckles of the left, or lower, hand. Actually, the second joints of the top hand tend to fall midway between the knuckles and second joints of the bottom hand. The grip should be firm but not rigid. In preparation for the forward swing

at the ball, the bat is held behind the rear shoulder with the rear arm bent, elbow pointing downward, and the forward arm extended back across the chest with wrists cocked. Since the objective of the swing is to hit the ball on a horizontal plane, the bat should be held on a plane more horizontal than vertical. The swing is initiated by a shift of weight to the forward foot, caused by a short step or sliding of the forward foot. The hips then rotate forward, preceding the shoulders and arms. The bat travels in an outward horizontal arc, the wrists uncocking at the moment of impact and rolling into the follow-through. The batter should permit the momentum of the bat to dissipate in the follow-through before releasing the bat.

Although beginners should have the experience of "swinging away," they should also experience swinging to meet and place the ball. In this case, the same grip and stance are used, with the exception that the hands are three to four inches from the butt

Fig. 7.10. Batting

end of the bat in a "choked up" grip in order to achieve greater control of the bat. The ball is met with this shortened grip over the front of the plate to send the ball to the left, and over the rear of the plate to send the ball to the right. Players can direct the ball to the ground more easily with this swing, as would be necessary in a hit-and-run situation.

PROGRESSION AND TEACHING SUGGESTIONS

The most common mistakes in batting are:

1. Swinging with the arms only, without shifting weight forward or rotating hips.
2. Not swinging on a level plane but chopping or "golfing" the swing.
3. Not uncocking the wrists and not rolling them over into the follow-through.
4. Not gripping the bat firmly enough, permitting energy dissipation at contact.
5. Swinging late at a fast-ball pitch.

Although the grip, stance, and swing are important in batting, success is achieved only when the swing is timed to the pitch. In all batting, the batter must perceive the speed and placement of the pitch. If the pitch is slow, the batter has the time to watch the ball in flight and make decisions. If the pitch is fast, the batter must start her swing with the release of the ball and has little time for last-minute adjustments. Batting from batting tees and slow pitching will help the batter organize her swing but will not help, and may hinder, her perception of a well-pitched ball. The faster the pitch, the farther the batter will be able to hit the ball. The level and skill of each performer should determine how she should practice batting skills.

DRILLS

1. Batting tees or a ball suspended on rope or wire can be used in early development of beginning batters. They have little value other than to help the participant get "the feel" of swinging and hitting the ball.
2. Pitching machines that can be adapted to softballs and used at different speeds are useful as a practice station.
3. Batting practice from a pitched ball is an effective practice for most players at most skill levels. The speed of the pitch should vary with the skill of the batter.
4. Combined drills incorporating pitching, batting, fielding, and throwing can be gamelike for small groups.

FIRST GAME SITUATIONS

The first regulation game situation in softball does not have the same elements of direct interaction of teams that occur in many of the other team sports. There is a clear definition between the offensive and defensive teams. If gamelike drills and modified games are a part of the experience of the participant, it is a relatively easy step to progress to the regulation game. Many teachers will find the need to make certain modifications in games for beginners in order to insure the greatest amount of participation by all and to maintain interest and enthusiasm. Too often, the regulation game can become a game of throw and catch between the pitcher and catcher, or a series of walks to successive batters, or one team dominating as the batting team. While playing the regulation game is important, there may be limitations for a group of beginners, and common sense must prevail. Some modifications might include:

1. Rotating all field positions, including pitcher and catcher, after each batter or series of batters.
2. Decreasing the number of balls and strikes for a walk or out.
3. Permitting all players on the batting team to bat and then changing sides regardless of number of outs.

Intermediate Skills

The skills in this section are not necessarily more difficult than those in the beginning skills section. They are considered intermediate because they are not absolutely required in order to play the game, yet are considered essential to the total game.

BUNTING

The bunt is a short surprise hit that is used to advance a runner on base or as an infield base hit. For a bunt to be successful, it must be deceptive and well placed.

The batter attempting to bunt should assume the same grip and stance as if she were going to hit the ball in the usual manner so as not to reveal her intentions. As the ball is released by the pitcher, the batter pivots on both feet to face the oncoming ball. At the same time, the bat is brought across the body, the top hand sliding approximately halfway up the bat. The remainder of the bat extends over the plate and *meets* the ball to direct it toward the ground down the first or third base line. The

Fig. 7.11. Bunting

grip should not be tense, and it should loosen on impact to cut down on the rebound of the ball.

PROGRESSION AND TEACHING SUGGESTIONS

The most common errors in bunting are:

1. Assuming the bunting stance too soon and not being deceptive.
2. Hitting or swinging at the ball.
3. Sending the ball into the air rather than on the ground.
4. Missing the ball because of the change in stance and position.

The bunt should not be introduced until the players have developed sufficient confidence in their batting skills. Bunting requires deception, and players are not cap-

able of deception until they have confidence in their skills. Drills should demand the practice of deception.

DRILLS

The drills for bunting are essentially the same as for batting. After the basic introduction and practice, the participants should practice with a pitcher, alternating full swings, place hits, and bunts.

BASERUNNING

Although baserunning is necessary at the beginning levels, particular skills and knowledge can be introduced after the first game situations. The major objective in baserunning is to get from one base to an-

Fig. 7.12. Baserunning—path of the base runner.

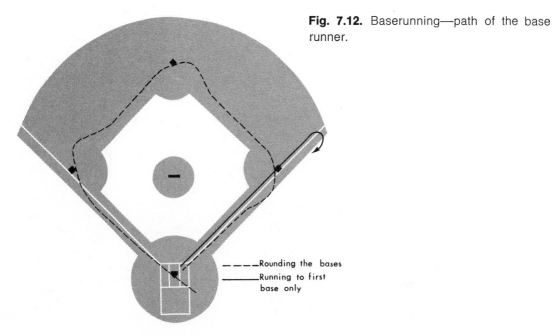

- - - - Rounding the bases
———— Running to first base only

other, or around one, two, or three bases, as quickly as possible.

The batter becomes a base runner upon hitting the ball. As the weight will be on the forward foot in the follow-through of the hit, the rear foot steps in a direct line toward first base. The first concern of the base runner is to get to first base as quickly as possible. Since *the rules permit overrunning first base without liability of being put out*, the runner should run directly to and *through* first base. The runner touches the outer half of the base with either foot without looking at the flight of the ball. When the ball is hit in such a way as to obviously be more than a one-base hit, or the first-base coach waves the player past first base, a slight outward arc should be made by the base runner before reaching the base. The base is then touched on the infield corner on the way toward second base. This outward curve is repeated at each base when the runner is continuing on to the next base. A direct line is taken when advancing only one base. *Once a player reaches first base, turns, and makes an advance toward second base, she forfeits the exemption from liability to be put out.*

PROGRESSION AND TEACHING SUGGESTIONS

The most common errors in baserunning are:

1. Waiting to see where the ball is hit before starting to first base.
2. Watching the ball while running to first base.
3. Stopping at the base and not overrunning first base on a one-base hit.
4. Being undecided whether or not to take another base.
5. Overrunning second or third base.

DRILLS

The best drill for baserunning is baserunning under game conditions. Other practices that can assist are the following:

1. Each player has a turn as batter and is timed with a stopwatch from the contact of the ball until either foot touches first base.
2. Same as number 1, with batter timed until she reaches second, third, or home.
3. Runner starts on first base and is timed until she reaches second base, without overrunning the base.

STEALING BASES

Stealing a base in softball is a method of advancing from one base to another without the benefit of a hit or a walk. *Base runners may advance, with liability of being put out, when the ball leaves the pitcher's hand.* This makes softball very different from baseball. The softball base runner may not lead off the base until the ball leaves the pitcher's hand.

The base runner attempting to steal second, third, or home must commit herself to the effort and cannot be indecisive. On each pitch, the base runner should have one foot touching the side of the base and be in a forward stride position toward the next base. As the ball leaves the pitcher's hand, the base runner starts quickly toward the next base. She should continue for three or four steps even if she has no intention of stealing. In this way she can capitalize on any mistake made by the catcher, such as a passed ball. Once the base runner has decided to steal, or has been coached to steal, she should start quickly toward the next base and continue, without watching the catcher, until she reaches the base. If the catcher does throw to the base she is attempting to reach, watching the ball may cause indecision and slow the base runner down. Until a player has learned to slide and is properly protected, she should concentrate on reaching the base, without overrunning, in a standing position.

PROGRESSION AND TEACHING SUGGESTIONS

The most common errors in stealing are:

1. Lack of an explosive start as the ball leaves the pitcher's hand.
2. Watching the ensuing play while attempting to steal.
3. Indecisiveness or slowing down, when stealing.

Stealing requires timing and a commitment to the act. It should not be assumed that all players know how to steal, since "no stealing" has been a modified rule imposed on many girls and women playing softball because of lack of backstops and lack of confidence in the ability of catchers and basemen.

DRILLS

The most effective practice for stealing is under gamelike conditions. With one team in the field, each member of the batting team is given the opportunity to start from first base and attempt to steal second, third, and home. The base runner can be instructed to steal on a particular pitch, for example, the third pitch, or decide on her own when to steal. Whether safe or out, the player continues until she attempts to steal home. During the first practice, it is recommended that the runner be given a specific pitch on which to steal. Otherwise, indecisive runners may never make the attempt.

During this practice, the batter should be instructed not to hit the pitches. This particular practice for stealing also provides an excellent opportunity for all members of the defensive team to experience the catcher's position.

Selected Advanced Skills

The following skills may not be taught in the regular instructional program. They are for the player who has mastered the beginning and intermediate levels and has the desire and ability to progress further. Progressions, teaching suggestions, and drills are presented only for skills that are unlike those presented in previous sections.

SLIDING

A player may slide into a base in order to avoid being tagged out when advancing from one base to another. Sliding is just what the name infers—the player slides along the ground the last few feet before a base in order to touch the base below a possible tag-out by the baseman. Since first base may be overrun without liability of being put out, a player should not slide into first base as it is far quicker to run through the base. It is unreasonable to expect a player to slide and unwise to practice sliding without the protection of long pants. Some competitors wear long socks for protection. This is inadequate for average players of varying skills and competence.

There are three basic types of slides: the straight-in, the bent-leg, and the hook. In all slides it is imperative that once the slide is begun, it be continued. Injury can result when a player changes her mind in the middle of a slide.

The *straight-in* slide begins with a backward lean and extension of one leg, usually the right, toward the base. The weight-bearing foot will begin to slide along the ground as the body approaches the horizontal. This leg should then be bent at the knee as the slide continues toward the base, and the toe of the extended leg touches the base.

The *bent-leg* slide, an adaptation of the straight-in slide, permits the runner to recover quickly in case there is an opportunity to advance farther. This slide begins a bit closer to the base, and the non-weight-bearing leg is not fully extended. As the toe of the leg touches the base, the weight is brought forward onto the knee of the sliding leg, thus permitting the runner to take a step with the nonsliding leg.

The *hook* slide is most often used when the runner is aware that the baseman already holds the ball and is waiting for the tag-out. The slide is approached in the same manner as the straight-in slide. As the extended leg approaches the base, the upper part of the body and the sliding leg are twisted away from the base to avoid the tag, and the toe of the extended leg "hooks" the base.

Since rubber- or metal-spiked shoes are often worn for softball, care must be taken that these spikes are clear of the ground on a slide. Raising the feet high is dangerous for the baseman. Even without spiked shoes, there is a concern about potential injury.

PROGRESSION AND TEACHING SUGGESTIONS

The most common errors in sliding are:

1. Starting the slide too late or too early, causing the runner to hit the base with too much force or not reaching the base by the end of the slide.
2. Being unsure whether or not to slide, and changing in the middle of the slide.

3. Lack of courage to slide at all and simply slowing down and being put out.
4. Throwing the body into a horizontal position or jumping into the slide.

Not all girls and women are "overjoyed" at the prospect of sliding into a base. This skill should be reserved for competitive play or for those who really wish to learn it.

DRILLS

It is often difficult to make the first slide. Because of the "courage" factor, it is suggested that the first attempts and practice not take place on a regulation field.

1. To acquire the feel of getting the body into a horizontal position and sliding, the following "soft" techniques may be used:

   a. Sliding in a sandpit
   b. Sliding on a long mat
   c. Sliding on grass

2. Sliding into a base—start at a reduced speed several steps away from the base and gradually increase the speed and distance before the slide is taken.

Because of possible irritation to the leg, sliding should not be practiced for long periods at any one time.

ADVANCED PITCHING

Once a pitcher has mastered the straight fast ball, she can attempt other pitches. A simple *change of pace* pitch is often confusing to the batter. The windup is the same as for the fast ball. The grip is basically the same, with the ball held loosely or with the fingertips. The change of pace is thrown with little or no spin imparted to the ball. Those with large hands may grip the ball with the knuckles of the fingers. If the player has small hands, the fingernails can assist her in gripping the ball. All four fingers release at the same time, and the thumb extends forward.

The *windmill delivery* can be deceptive to the batter and permits greater momentum to be imparted to the ball. The delivery starts from the same basic stance as that for the slingshot delivery. The pitching arm moves forward and upward as the shoulders and hips rotate backward. As the pitching arm moves through the full circle, the opposite foot lifts off the rubber in preparation for the forward step. The pitching arm is

extended and gains momentum as it passes overhead. On the downward swing, the step is taken with the opposite foot, and the ball is released as the foot of the pitching arm pushes off the rubber. The follow-through is the same as in the slingshot delivery.

The *drop pitch* is one in which the ball breaks downward as it reaches the plate. The object is to impart forward spin to the ball. This is accomplished either with the usual fast-ball grip, with the fingers snapping upward and the thumb releasing first, or by holding the ball as if flipping a marble.

An *in* or *out curve* is one in which the ball breaks to the right or left. A curve can

be attempted with the fast-ball grip by snapping the wrist in the direction of the intended curve.

As a pitcher begins to work on various pitches, she will find modifications of the basic grips that will enable her to pitch different pitches most effectively. It will take a number of seasons of intensive practice to develop any real degree of success with the more advanced pitches.

ADVANCED THROWS

The *sidearm throw* is used most often by infielders fielding a ground ball when there is a close play involved and there is not time to make an overarm throw. The throwing arm is brought back low from the low catch, and in the throwing action the forearm is parallel to the ground. The sidearm action tends to bring the arm across the body in the follow-through, and the flight of the ball will tend to be from right to left for a right-handed thrower. To counteract this action, the wrist snap should be in the direction the ball is to travel, rather than in the more natural action across the body. When the forearm falls below a line parallel to the ground on the throw, it becomes an *underhand whip throw*.

Fig. 7.13. Windmill delivery.

The catcher should have an overhand throw that does not require a full windup. This type of throw is called an *overhand snap throw*. The pattern is similar to that of the basic overhand throw except that the take-back is closer to the ear, the windup shorter, and the force is imparted primarily through a strong wrist snap rather than a full arm action.

STRATEGY

The team in the field is on the defense, while the team at bat is on the offense. Softball has very little direct interaction between the two teams.

Softball consists of seven innings, each team alternately at bat. When each team has had one turn at bat, one inning has been completed. The offensive team attempts to score as many runs as possible before three outs are committed. The defensive team attempts to make three outs on the offensive team as quickly as possible and before any runs have been scored. It is toward these respective ends that all strategy is aimed.

Because of the nature of this book, only basic strategy will be presented. It must be remembered, however, that basic strategy and skills are *basic* to *all* levels of play.

Offensive Strategy

Offensive strategy is primarily a combination of batting and baserunning.

The *batting order* of the team is determined by the relative strengths of the hitters. It is arranged in such a way as to "bunch" the hits and thereby score runs. The leadoff or first batter is a player who can consistently get on base. She is usually not a long-ball hitter, but a good single hitter, who draws walks often, and has the speed to "beat out" infield hits. The second batter is a good place hitter and bunter. She should have the ability to advance the runner on base to the next base whether or not she is out herself. The third batter is a hitter who can consistently hit to the outfield with some degree of power. The fourth batter or "clean up" hitter is the longest and strongest hitter on the team. This hitter has the potential to score the players on base by hitting extra base hits. The fifth batter is the strongest of the remaining hitters, with diminishing power in the remaining players down to the ninth batter. The pitcher is often placed in last position, but she should be judged on her batting merits when playing in the offensive lineup.

Softball offensive plays, rather than players doing whatever seems feasible at the time, demand that the batter and base runners know what is about to be attempted. For this reason, in competitive play, the offensive plays are signaled to the batter and base runners by *base coaches*. The third-base coach usually determines the play. The use of base coaches to determine what the batter and base runners will do in beginning play is a questionable practice. Beginners often have difficulty in hitting the ball at all. To require them to hit a specific pitch or let a specific pitch go by takes decision-making away from the player and may dampen enthusiasm and discourage the beginner. However, base coaches can assist the base runners by indicating when they can advance more than one base on a hit (waving a player on), when they should hold a base, and when they can leave the base on a sacrifice fly. It is obvious, as players become more skilled, that confusion can result without base coaches, if only to relay the intentions of the batter to the base runners or vice versa. For example, if a base runner is attempting to steal and the batter is unaware of this intent and hits a fly ball to the infield, the attempted steal, in this case, is sure to cause another out if the ball is caught. If the batter had been aware of the steal, she would let the pitch go by or would have swung with no intention of hitting the ball in order to confuse the catcher.

The number of balls and strikes, or *count*, on a batter can determine what she will do. If the count is 3–0 (3 balls, no strikes), it may be advisable not to swing on the next pitch as the odds are good for a walk. Conversely, the pitcher has the advantage over the batter on an 0–2 count. The batter must be careful not to swing at a pitch that will be a ball, but she must swing at any pitch she feels may be a strike. In effect, each batter constitutes a game within the game.

Particular offensive strategies include place hitting, hit and run, stealing, bunting, sacrifice bunt or fly, and squeeze play.

Place hitting is hitting the ball, usually with a slightly "choked" grip, to some specific, predetermined area of the field. Place hitting is usually an attempt for a single and is also used in the hit and run play. The *hit and run* play is an attempt to move the base runners one base, and preferably two, on the hit. When the hit and run play is on, the base runner, usually on first base, leaves with the pitch for second base as in the steal. The batter attempts to hit the ball, no matter how bad the pitch, on the ground *behind* the runner. The reasons for hitting behind the runner are to avoid hitting the base runner with the ball and to make it a difficult throw to get the base runner out, as most fielders are right-handed. The hit

and run can be dangerous strategy as the chance for a double play is great, and if the batter misses the ball, the runner may be put out in an attempted steal.

Stealing is a means of advancing the runner or runners without the benefit of a hit or walk. If two runners steal at the same time, this is called a *double steal*. When to steal is determined by a number of variables. If the catcher does not have an accurate or quick throw, the runners may find stealing quite effective—particularly to second base as this is the longest throw for the catcher. If there are less than two outs and runners on first and third bases, the runner stealing second may not even draw a throw from the catcher since the runner on third might easily score. If the second baseman and shortstop are drawn out of position and cannot cover the base in case of a steal, the runner should attempt a steal. In all cases, the runner must have the ability to move quickly. A thrown ball moves much faster than a running player.

A *bunt* can be used for a variety of reasons. A good bunter and fast runner can attempt to bunt against a deep infield for a base hit. The bunt can also be used as a sacrifice out to advance a base runner. In this case, the batter must make every attempt to run out the hit, as the object of the sacrifice bunt is to draw the throw for the possible out at first base and thus discourage an attempt to put out the runner going to second base. The base runner on second base is now in position to score on a single.

The same is true of the *sacrifice fly*. The batter attempts to hit long. If the long hit is a fly ball that is caught, the *base runner may advance after the catch but must first touch the base she was on at the time of the hit.*

GENERAL OFFENSIVE STRATEGY

1. Base runners must be alert at all times and lead off with each pitch.
2. Base runners should not overrun second and third bases unless they are going on to the next base.
3. On a fly ball, when there are fewer than two outs, base runners should advance about halfway to the next base until the ball is caught or missed.
4. On any hit with two outs, the base runners should run to the next base on the pitch regardless of the type of hit.
5. If the base runners are alert, there should never be an occasion when two base runners occupy the same base. If this does occur, the object is not to cause an out. Either the lead runner must advance or the trailing runner must retreat.
6. In the case of a rundown (a player caught off base between two fielders), the base runner should cause as many throws as possible to increase the chance for error and attempt to get to either base, whichever one permits her to be safe.
7. If the base runner realizes that she can reach a base safely, she should round the base, evaluate the position of the ball and defensive players, and continue running if there is an error or if the next base cannot be covered.
8. The base runner should be ready to capitalize on any errors made by the defensive team (e.g., a passed ball, a wild pitch, or an outfielder holding the ball).
9. If the pitcher is erratic or lacks control, the batter should be very selective about swinging at pitches.
10. With a good fast-ball pitcher, the batter should choke up on her grip to enable a faster swing and try to "meet" the ball.
11. On any contact with the ball, the batter should run as fast as possible to and through first base without watching the progress of the ball.

Defensive Strategy

Defensive strategy consists primarily of pitching, positioning, catching, and throwing the ball.

Basic positioning and the areas of coverage of each fielder are shown in figure 7.14. The back or regular positioning is used when there is no one on base or if there are two outs. If there are runners on base and less than two outs, all infielders move in a few steps from the back position. The close position is used when there is a runner on third and less than two outs or when the infield suspects a bunt.

Good positioning and alertness on the part of each fielder are necessary on each pitch. If the batter hits the ball, the fielders must know who is to attempt to handle it and where it should be thrown. The players not directly involved in fielding the ball should be *backing up* the play. In general, if the ball is hit to left or right field, the center fielder backs up the player fielding the ball. If the center fielder is fielding the ball, the closest outfielder will back up the play. On a batted ball to the infield, the closest outfielder should be moving in to back up the infielder. Backing up on the initial fielding of the ball is an attempt to be in position to handle the ball if the fielder misses or misplays it. After the initial fielding, the ball will be thrown to a base which involves

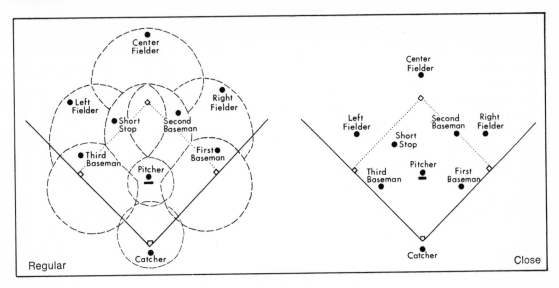

Fig. 7.14. Defense positioning

further backing up should the player miss the catch. At this point, players may have to *cover* bases that are different from their original positions. On a bunt, the first baseman, third baseman, or catcher will field the ball, the pitcher or second baseman will cover first base, and the shortstop or left fielder will cover third base. If there is a runner on third base, the pitcher will cover home plate if the catcher is fielding the ball. Every batted ball and every runner on base can provide a unique situation for backing up and covering. Fielders must have enough understanding of the game to know what can happen, where the ball will be thrown, what the runners are likely to do, and then to act accordingly. Each play should be backed up from beginning to end and all necessary bases covered.

On long hits to the outfield, a *relay throw* may be necessary. Generally, the shortstop, second baseman, or first baseman will move slightly out toward the outfielder to relay the throw, depending on where the ball has been hit. The relay throw is used when the outfielder cannot reach the infield with her throw.

DUTIES OF SPECIFIC POSITIONS

PITCHER   The pitcher should possess a high degree of accuracy in pitching. She must be able to pitch consistently over the plate within the strike zone of the batter in such a way that the batter has difficulty in hitting the ball. Pitchers are "made" not born. Good pitching requires a great deal of practice. A pitcher should first master a fast-ball pitch and learn to control high and low pitches. Her windup for each pitch should look the same so as to deceive the batter. She should concentrate on the plate and the strike zone, and not on the batter. She should try to analyze the batter and pitch accordingly. For example, pitch inside to a batter who crowds the plate; pitch outside to the batter who stands far away from the plate; pitch a fast ball to a slow swinger or a batter standing forward in the batter's box; pitch a slow ball to the fast swinger or a batter deep in the batter's box; and pitch high to a potential bunter.

The pitcher must be in position to field after each pitch and be ready to assume covering and backing up duties. The pitcher may cover first base on a hit toward first base. She must cover home plate on a wild pitch, passed ball, or if the catcher is out of position and there is a runner on third.

CATCHER   This is one of the most demanding positions on the field. Before the pitch, the catcher assumes an easy squat position, at which time she gives signals to the pitcher, if this is the plan. In preparation for the pitch, she raises slightly from the full squat to a semi-squat position with her feet in a diagonal stride. The catcher's mitt should be a stationary target for the pitcher. Her bare hand should be close to the mitt in a fist or with fingers close together. *The catcher must be within the catcher's box and cannot interfere with the batter's swing.* It is most important that the catcher not close her eyes or shy away if the batter swings or as the ball enters her mitt. For this reason, not everyone can be a successful catcher. If the pitch is wide, high, or low, the catcher must move to attempt to catch the ball. If she cannot catch it, every attempt should be made to block the ball so that it does not get behind her and become a passed ball. The catcher should flip off her

Fig. 7.15. The catcher

Before the pitch

On the pitch

mask before fielding the ball or backing up a play. The chest protector is not removed during a play. The catcher should be able to reach each base from home plate with an overhead snap throw.

FIRST BASEMAN   The first baseman should have exceptional ability in catching all types of throws. The majority of throws to a base, in most games, are to first base. The first baseman is positioned toward second base and behind the base path when no one is on first base and it is not a bunt situation. With a runner on first base, the first baseman should position herself closer to the base for a possible pick-off throw. In a bunting situation, she positions in front of the base.

When the ball is thrown to first base, the baseman reaches for the ball, the familiar

term *stretch*, so as to catch it at the first possible moment, and extends her opposite foot to touch the base.

SECOND BASEMAN   The second baseman should be able to field on both sides and have an accurate, quick throw. Her basic position is on the first-base side of second base and behind the base path. Basically, the second baseman is responsible for fielding all balls hit in her area, covering second base on a steal, and covering second when the ball is hit to another fielder. In some cases, she may cover first base if the first baseman is fielding the ball. Covering the base when a player is stealing or attempting second when not forced requires certain positioning for the tag play. The baseman moves to a position straddling the base and facing the incoming runner. She rotates her upper body in the direction of the throw, catches the ball, and swings the glove down to tag the runner. In a double-play situation, the second baseman will field the ball, if it is in her area, and throw to the shortstop covering second base. If another player is fielding the ball, the second baseman should time her run to the base so that she catches the ball as her foot touches the base. She immediately pivots and throws to first base.

SHORTSTOP   The shortstop should be very quick and agile and should possess a strong, quick throw. She is positioned between second and third bases and behind the base path. Since the majority of players are right-handed, the shortstop will have many balls hit toward her position. She must be able to field ground and bouncing balls and throw quickly to first base. When the second baseman is fielding the ball or covering first base, the shortstop assumes the duties of covering second base. The shortstop may also be called upon to back up the pitcher

Fig. 7.16. Covering first base

on a hit to the box, cover third base if the third baseman is fielding a bunt, back up the third baseman on a play at third, and receive a relay throw from the outfield.

THIRD BASEMAN   The third baseman should have a strong, long throw. She will be called upon to field a ball behind third base and throw the width of the diamond to first base. The third baseman is positioned on the second-base side and behind the base path. With a player on second or third, she will move closer to the base. In a bunt situation, she moves in toward home plate in front of the base path. Most outs at third base are tag plays, and she must be able to cover the base in the same manner described for the second baseman in this situation.

OUTFIELDERS   The three outfielders must have the ability to judge the direction and the distance the ball will travel as it is being hit. Literally, on the crack of the bat the outfielders must be off to the best position to intercept the ball. The outfielders position according to the batter and the situation. With weak batters they move in; with strong batters they move out. With a left-handed batter they move around toward the first-base line, and with a right-handed "pull" hitter they move toward the third-base line. The closest outfielder backs up the one making the play, and each outfielder backs up the infielders playing in front of her. The outfielders will be called upon to field long fly balls, short fly balls, hard-hit drives, bouncing balls, and ground balls. In all cases, they must make the catch quickly and throw the ball to the infield. Before the catch is made, the fielder must have evaluated the situation and decided to which base or player to throw. In the case of a long hit, she should look for the infielder coming out to relay the ball.

GENERAL DEFENSIVE STRATEGY

1. Try to put out the advance runner (the one closest to home plate) whenever possible.
2. When it is not possible to put out the advance runner, attempt to get the most advanced runner that is a sure out.
3. With two outs, go for the sure out— usually first base.
4. Each fielder should be ready to move on each pitch. Never hesitate to field a ball.
5. Fielders should be encouraged to call out "Mine" or "I've got it" or to give some appropriate signal when attempting to field fly balls. A fielder hearing the call should move off the catch in order to avoid a collision.
6. Although pitching is a very important part of defense, fielders must realize the importance of their individual roles.

BASIC UNIT PLAN FOR BEGINNERS

The following brief outline of an eighteen-lesson unit plan assumes that the instructor will select areas for review in which students need practice. It is suggested that the students warm up each day, using the skills of the game. One method is to set up stations with specific tasks designed to promote skill development. This cannot logically occur until some basic skills are presented. The stations can utilize tasks of a skill test nature so that students can determine and evaluate their own progress.

Although officiating, rules, and strategy appear in the unit plan, a great amount of the information should be covered as the situations occur in play and practice.

Lesson 1   Wearing a glove—catching —fielding

SELECTED BIBLIOGRAPHY

AMATEUR SOFTBALL ASSOCIATION. *Official Guide.* Available: 4515 North Santa Fe, Oklahoma City, Okla. 73118. Published each year.

DIVISION FOR GIRLS AND WOMEN'S SPORTS. *Softball Guide.* Washington, D.C.: AAHPER. Published every two years.

KNEER, MARIAN, ed. *Selected Softball Articles.* Washington, D.C.: AAHPER., 1962.

KNEER, MARIAN, and McCORD, CHARLES. *Softball.* Dubuque, Ia.: Wm. C. Brown Co. Publishers, 1966.

Volleyball

Volleyball has been a popular recreational sport for girls and women for many years. The game was developed in 1895 for men participating in YMCA programs as a less strenuous game than basketball. Women soon adapted the men's rules, and the first rules specifically for women were published in 1926. Although a United States invention, volleyball has enjoyed greater popularity as a competitive sport abroad than in the United States. The inclusion of women's volleyball in the 1964 Olympics was responsible for many rapid changes in the nature of the game in the United States. Prior to 1964, only a few players in this country were engaged in highly skilled competition. Since 1964, when other countries, notably the Japanese national team, demonstrated the high level of skill existing outside the United States, the development of volleyball has soared. Instructional programs in schools, colleges, and clubs have veered sharply away from "mass" volleyball requiring little physical conditioning and skill toward the concept of "power" volleyball. While the power volleyball skills are necessary for highly skilled play, they are recognized as basic skills for all levels of play.

There are two major rule-making bodies for volleyball for girls and women. Schools and colleges usually conduct play under the rules published by the Division for Girls and Women's Sports (DGWS) of the American Association for Health, Physical Education, and Recreation. Other competitive groups outside the educational institutions conduct play most frequently under the United States Volleyball Association (USVBA) rules. The differences in the two sets of rules have been greatly reduced in recent years, and it is anticipated that continued cooperative efforts will eventually produce one set of rules.

EQUIPMENT

Balls

A laceless, leather-covered ball is required by the rules for indoor play. The ball should be inflated to seven or eight pounds of air pressure for official play. While rubber-covered balls are permitted for outdoor play, tend to stand up well, and require little care, they are not recommended for indoor use. Rubber balls become very smooth or slick with use and are slippery if damp. They tend to sting the arms and fingers more than the leather-covered balls. Beginners are quickly aware of differing amounts of sting of the two types of balls, and their exposure to the game should be as positive as possible. More advanced players prefer the "feel" of the leather balls.

Leather balls should be used on smooth surfaces only, as the leather will cut or become roughened on cement or asphalt. The ball can be cleaned periodically with saddle soap.

Nets and Standards

The official net is thirty-two feet long and three feet wide. For official play, the top of the net is seven feet four and one-quarter inches from the ground. While ropes are usually used to suspend the net for instructional play, the rules require wire cables for official play. Whatever the requirements of the situation, it is important that the net be tightly stretched, by the four corners, between standards that are well outside the court. Standards of varying types are available. The major concerns are that the stan-

dards be well outside the sidelines; that the standards be fastened securely into the floor, and if guide wires or support cables are used, that they not be a potential hazard for the players; that the bases of the standards be as flat as possible; and that any protruding parts, for example, cranks, be removable, collapsible, or padded. Even for the instructional situation, the nets should be taut and properly secured. Drooping, sagging nets do not encourage good play.

Nets can be folded for storage and should be repaired immediately when a cord is broken or frayed. Nets should not be stored in boxes or bags with leather balls, as the nets may stain the balls.

Court and Markings

The court is sixty feet long by thirty feet wide. It is recommended that the ceiling be thirty feet high or more. It is important that there be adequate space on all sides and backs of the court to permit players to play a ball that may have been sent out-of-

Fig. 8.1. Court and markings

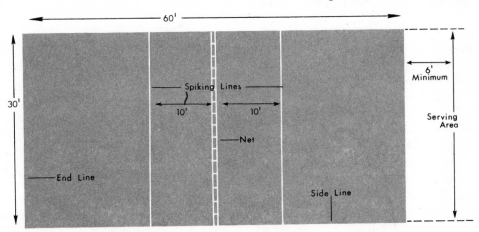

bounds by a teammate. Floor surfaces should be clean and dry.

Uniforms

Clothing that permits freedom of movement is necessary for volleyball. The typical uniform is short or stretch shorts and shirt. Long-sleeved shirts may be worn to protect the arms from floor burns and the impact of the ball. One-piece uniforms may not permit the necessary freedom of movement. Footwear should permit good traction with the floor and little sliding of the foot inside the shoe.

Knee Pads

Although it may not be practical or possible for instructional classes, if players are expected to contact the floor with their knees, they should wear protective knee pads. Certainly they are a must for competitive play.

UNDERLYING SKILL REQUIREMENTS

Volleyball requires quick reaction time, speed, agility, and a certain degree of strength. Although it is not basically a running game, it does require conditioning in terms of short, quick moves, bending low, jumping high, and being able to repeat these moves in quick succession over a period of time. A certain degree of strength is necessary to effectively spike, block, set, and serve overhead.

A hard-hit spike or serve may be threatening to some girls and women. They must be prepared psychologically to meet the hard-hit ball without ducking or closing their eyes and with skills that permit the handling of such balls.

SKILLS

Volleyball skills are divided into beginning, intermediate, and advanced. The basic skills necessary to play a regulation game are considered beginning skills, although they remain basic to the game at all levels. Intermediate skills are those skills that are appropriate for and enhance beginning play but are not absolutely required for a first game situation. Advanced skills may or may not be taught in a basic instructional program and are the skills for those players who are competent in the beginning and intermediate skills. Within each section, the skills are presented in a general progression. Each skill is described in terms of its use, analyzed, and followed by common errors and teaching suggestions. Drills are included for each skill or group of similar skills. Modified and first game experiences are included where appropriate.

Beginning Skills

The skills necessary to play the game are a serve and some means of playing the ball above the head and below the head.

FOREARM PASS

The forearm pass, also called forearm bump, dig, or bounce pass, is used in a variety of situations when the ball is below head level. The ball is allowed to rebound off both forearms simultaneously with little chance of an illegal hit. It is particularly useful in receiving a serve or spike where an overhead hit is likely to result in a ball-handling violation. The forearm pass is not as accurate as the overhead pass and should not be used if the overhead pass is possible.

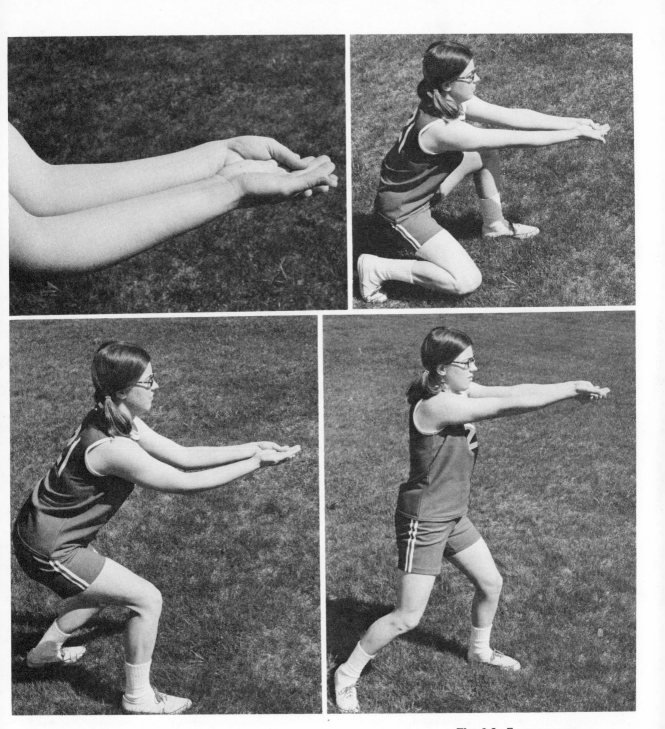

Fig. 8.2. Forearm pass

As the ball is put in play, all players should be in a position ready to play the ball. In this *ready position*, the player is in a forward stride position with weight forward, arms and hands low with palms up. From this position the player can move left, right, forward, or back, depending on the flight of the ball and the play. As the ball approaches, the player should be in line with and behind the ball. Most highly skilled players agree that a forward stride position is preferred to a side stride position, as the former provides a base of support in the direction of the flight of the ball and permits last-minute correction of body position if necessary. The knees and ankles flex to permit the body to be lowered according to the flight of the ball. The forearms are away from the body at a forty-five-degree angle to the floor. The hands are clasped with the both palms facing upward. The forearms are rotated outward, presenting the largest and flattest surface of the arms to the ball. The arms are not swung upward to meet the ball. Rather, the knees and ankles extend, causing the arms to contact the ball. With the upward motion, the wrists hyperextend, and the elbows extend with forearms parallel. The ball is contacted approximately midway between the wrists and elbows of both arms simultaneously. After contact, the extension of the legs continues with little upward follow-through of the arms.

PROGRESSION AND TEACHING SUGGESTIONS

The most common errors in the forearm pass are:

1. Swinging the arms upward to hit the ball, resulting in too hard a hit or an uncontrolled hit.

2. Having one forearm higher than another, resulting in a double hit or a misdirected ball.
3. Contacting the ball too close to the body, resulting in a misdirected ball.
4. Contacting the ball too far away from the body, resulting in contacting the ball on the hands or a weak hit.

Players will need practice with a variety of speeds and trajectories of the ball. Negating spin, the ball will rebound at an equal and opposite angle from its approach. The natural tendency is to swing at the ball, sending it high and wide. While this might be great fun, it will make for poor volleyball. Another difficulty that will be encountered is the discrimination between those balls that are best handled with the forearm pass and those that can be handled with the overhead pass. It must be remembered that the forearm pass is most effective for those balls that might otherwise result in illegal hits, that is, receiving the serve, receiving a spike, and balls below head level. Whenever possible, players should use the overhead pass, as it is more accurate than the forearm pass.

DRILLS

In each drill for a pass, the player should have someone or someplace be the object of the pass. Passing without an object is aimless and does not give feedback to the performer as to how well she has performed. In each case, the purpose is to get the ball up in the air in such a way that another player can handle it.

1. In twos or small groups, one player throws a soft high pass to another player who returns the ball with a forearm pass.

2. In twos or small groups, one player throws the ball slightly left or right, then short or long, to another player who returns the ball with a forearm pass.

3. In twos or small groups, the speed of the ball is increased on the throw, with variations of placement.

OVERHEAD PASS

The overhead is the best controlled accurate pass and is used most often as a "set" for the spiker. Although it is a controlled hit, it can result in an illegal hit when used to receive a spike, serve, or when the passer is not in a balanced and prepared position. In all hits, *the ball must be given immediate impetus at contact:** The flight of the ball is usually a high arch. Variations in the trajectory of sets can be attempted after players have mastered the basic pass.

* Italics indicate rules that determine the performance of a skill.

Fig. 8.3. Overhead pass

As the ball approaches, it is most important that the player be in the best possible position. This is the basic ready position as described for the forearm pass except that the hands are up approximately between the player's forehead and the expected downward arc of the ball. The fingers are spread but relaxed, pointed diagonally toward the ball with the thumbs pointed inward. The wrists are hyperextended, and the elbows are away from the body. Just before the ball is contacted, the knees begin to extend, and the hands move toward the ball so that it is contacted approximately eight inches away from the forehead. The ball is contacted with the pads of the fingertips and the second joint of the fingers. On contact, the knees continue to extend, along with a rapid extension of the elbows and a slight flexion of the wrists from the previously hyperextended position to a position of extension. After contact, the elbows continue to full extension, the arms and hands in the direction of the pass.

PROGRESSION AND TEACHING SUGGESTIONS

The most common errors in the overhead pass are:

1. Jumping at the ball, resulting in an inaccurate pass.
2. Keeping the elbows close to the body, resulting in restricted movement and an inaccurate pass.
3. Playing the ball too close to the body, resulting in a weak and inaccurate pass.
4. Attempting to play the ball off the ends of the fingers rather than the pads and second joint, resulting in a weak pass and possible injury.
5. Pulling the hands back quickly after contact to avoid an illegal hit, resulting in a weak hit.

Players often have many misconceptions about the overhead pass. Since the possibility of an illegal hit is often stressed, players may attempt many different "cures" for the malady, for example, pulling the hands away from the ball rather than following through. Because some players experience difficulty in gaining power in the beginning, they may jump at the ball or jump after hitting the ball. Watching more experienced players, beginners may incorrectly deduce that these players achieve power by pushing with their thumbs and may attempt to do this in their play.

The development of a spiking offense is hinged on the overhead pass, and time must be spent in developing this skill. Correct positioning is absolutely essential. A deeper knee bend may be used to contact a ball below normal forehead level, but too deep a bend will produce a push, and the forearm pass should be used instead.

DRILLS

1. In twos or small groups in a circle, one player tosses a softly arched ball to another player who passes the ball back to the thrower.
2. In twos or small groups in a circle, one player tosses a softly arched ball to the right or left of another player who passes the ball back to the thrower.
3. Each player with a ball or one player at a time within a group throws the ball up in the air to herself and attempts to repeatedly and successively pass the ball to herself. Adequate space must be available for each player to move to play the ball.
4. In twos or small groups, players attempt to continue passing to each other as many times as possible. At this point,

players must differentiate between the use of the forearm pass and the overhead pass. A competition can be developed between groups within a set time period. Each group counts the number of consecutive passes, or in the case of younger beginners, the number of successful passes whether consecutive or not. The time period should be sufficiently long to encourage the use of high sets.

MODIFIED GAME

In groups of six, basic offensive and defensive positioning, court play, and rotation can begin. The players have not learned a legal means for putting the ball into play, but a throw can be substituted for a serve. With six players on each side of the court, the ball is thrown by the "server" in the right back position. The receiving team attempts to receive the "serve" with a forearm pass directed toward the center forward position. Whether or not the pass actually reaches the center forward, she or the player in best position to play the ball attempts an overhead pass to a forward who attempts to send an overhead pass deep into the opponent's court. Basic scoring, rotation, and serving order are used as in the official game. This gets the players into the game quickly and establishes patterns for future play and, in addition, shows them the purpose of the skills they have learned up to this point.

UNDERHAND SERVE

The underhand serve is useful for beginning play but lacks the force and has too high a trajectory for use as an *offensive* serve at higher levels. Since some players

Fig. 8.4. Underhand serve

in a regular instructional class may experience difficulty with an overhand serve, the underhand serve can be introduced, giving everyone some means of serving the ball. It is recommended that the overhand serve be introduced as soon as possible so that the serve can become an offensive rather than a defensive skill. With true beginners, even an underhand serve may be difficult to receive and pass accurately.

The server begins behind the end line facing the net. The ball is held in the palm of the nonstriking hand about waist level in front of the server. In preparation for the hit, the striking arm swings straight back. As the striking arm begins its forward swing, a step with the foot opposite the striking arm is taken in the direction of the net. The ball is contacted on the lower half with the heel of the hand, a cupped palm, or the inside surface formed by closing the fingers into the palm, thumb to the side. *The rules under which play is conducted determine whether the ball may be hit directly off the palm of the nonstriking hand or whether the supporting hand must be quickly removed or the ball tossed prior to contact.* As the ball is contacted, the striking arm follows through in the direction of the hit, and the player steps into the court in position to play the return. Because the ball is hit from below the waist, the trajectory is rather high to enable the ball to clear the net and fall deep in the opponent's court.

PROGRESSION AND TEACHING SUGGESTIONS

The most common errors in performing the underhand serve are:

1. Throwing the ball out too far or allowing the ball to dribble off the ends of the fin-

gers of the supporting hand, resulting in a weak or missed serve.
2. Contacting the bottom of the ball above waist height, sending it straight up or too high.
3. Contacting the ball on the forearm, resulting in an inaccurate serve.
4. Attempting to punch at the ball rather than swinging the striking arm in an arc.
5. Mistiming the swing or throw and not hitting the ball squarely or missing the ball entirely.

The underhand serve can be very accurate. However, it is difficult to achieve a great amount of force and still clear the net or keep the ball within the opponent's court. The server should attempt to keep the ball as low as possible, yet cause the ball to go over the net deep into the opponent's court or to a space left uncovered. It is more difficult to hit a ball tossed in the air than to hit a ball directly out of the supporting hand. If the rules require that the ball be off the supporting hand, care must be taken to prevent the players from simply shooting the ball forward in time with the forward swing of the striking arm. This often results in a complete miss or, at best, a weak hit. A variation of this error may cause the frustrated player to attempt to "help" the hit by simultaneously throwing with the supporting hand while contacting with the striking hand. To alleviate or possibly prevent incorrect mechanics, the beginning server should practice first against a wall or some type of backstop rather than being confronted by the actual court and net. This permits the player to concentrate on the mechanics rather than on measuring success solely on whether or not the ball goes over the net. The distance from the wall and the height at which the ball should hit the wall can be increased until the player is actually hitting the distance and height required on the regulation court. In this way, players can progress at their own rate rather than immediately being presented with the seemingly impossible task of hitting the ball thirty feet and over the net. While basic volleyball skills may seem very easy to some, observation of typical beginning instructional classes reveal that there are some girls and women lacking in strength, and similar skill experiences, who may find the timing and force of the hit of a volleyball serve a difficult skill to produce. Early success of some type is important, particularly for the lesser skilled individual. However, early success should not be at the expense of the proper mechanics of the skill.

DRILLS

1. Each player with a ball, in twos or small groups, serves to a wall area ten to fifteen feet away. Increase the distance and height of the ball but not higher than will be required on the court.
2. In partners, one serves to the other across the net. If appropriate, each can start by standing about mid court, gradually moving back to the end line.

FIRST GAME SITUATION

The first regulation game situation becomes an extension of the earlier modified game. Through the modified game, the players should understand the basic concepts of offensive and defensive positioning, rotation, scoring, and the basic pattern of play. At this point, the serve is added, making the game regulation at this level. Basic concepts

are stressed, and players should see the development of the basic pattern of forearm pass, the set, and the hit to send the ball into the opponent's court. Hopefully, they should begin to feel the need for a more aggressive or offensive hit when sending the ball into the opponent's court—the *spike*. They will also be attempting to cope with other situations for which they are not prepared, for example, net recovery and balls that cannot be reached with two hands. This should spur interest in the skills to follow in the intermediate section. Meanwhile, however, they are playing a regulation game.

Intermediate Skills

The following skills are not required to play a regulation game, but players will find that these skills enable them to cope with a greater variety of situations and allow them to play more skillfully.

OVERHAND SERVE

The overhand serve, although more difficult to perform than the underhand serve, is much more effective as an offensive technique. Greater force can be transmitted to the ball, and the trajectory is low. With practice, the serve can be extremely accurate and deceptive. There are two basic types of overhand serves: the top spin serve and the floater serve. The top spin serve occurs more naturally than the floater serve when players first learn an overarm pattern for the serve.

The server stands behind the end line, facing the net in a forward stride position so that she may take a step forward without stepping on the line. The ball is held in front of the server at chest level with two

Fig. 8.5. Overhand serve

hands on opposite sides of the ball or with the nonstriking hand under the ball, the striking hand supporting on the top. With the weight on the rear foot, the ball is tossed up in front of the shoulder of the striking arm. The accuracy of the toss is most important, just as in the tennis serve. The ball must be thrown high enough so that it may be contacted with an almost fully extended arm after it has reached its peak and is on the way down. As the ball is released about head height, the shoulder of the striking arm rotates back, bringing the striking arm back with the upper arm approximately parallel to the ground, elbow flexed approximately ninety degrees, and wrist slightly hyperextended, hand open. As the ball reaches the top of the throw, a step forward is taken with the nonstriking-side foot, and the hips lead a rotation of the shoulders forward. The striking arm follows with the elbow leading. Just prior to contact, the elbow extends, and the ball is then contacted with the heel of the hand below the middle of the ball. The wrist snaps forward, and the fingers contact the ball, sending the ball forward and slightly up. The striking arm follows through in the direction of the ball, and the player steps into the court ready to play the return. The ball will travel in a straight path, and the top spin will cause the ball to drop.

The floater serve is basically the same pattern as the top spin serve except that no spin is imparted to the ball. The initial toss must be made slightly farther away from the player with a "dead," no-spin ball and the valve stem facing the player. Contact is made with the heel of the hand slightly below the middle of the ball on the valve stem. The wrist is *not* snapped forward but kept in the slightly hyperextended position. The follow-through is not as great as in the top spin serve but again in the direction of the ball. The trajectory of the serve will be slightly higher than the top spin serve, and because no spin is imparted to the ball, it will appear to "float" as it travels in the air, often moving erratically left, right, up, or down, making it a difficult serve to receive.

PROGRESSION AND TEACHING SUGGESTIONS

The most common errors in the overhand serves are:

1. Lack of accuracy and consistency in the toss-up, resulting in weak into-the-net or out-of-bounds serves.
2. Mistiming the step and swing with the toss of the ball.
3. Not hitting the ball squarely, resulting in a weak and inaccurate serve.
4. Punching at the ball rather than swinging the arm through.

The ball toss is a crucial element of the serve. Beginners tend to throw the ball too high or too low. If the ball is thrown too high, the player may mistime her swing while having to wait for the ball. If the ball is thrown too low, it is not possible to extend the elbow on contact. Beginners may also toss the ball off to the right or left, making an accurate serve difficult. Practice should be devoted to the ball toss to develop a consistent pattern. Beginners may attempt to hit the ball with little or no body action. The top spin serve particularly requires hip and shoulder action, coupled with a shift of weight to the forward foot. Players may become discouraged with the early results of their attempts with the overhand serve. Similarities to other overarm patterns should be stressed, indicating the *differences* in the length of the lever arm and the force at impact.

DRILLS

The drills listed for the underhand serve can be used for practice of the overhand serve as well. These include the use of a wall or backboard for early practice, increasing the distance as competence permits, and practice between partners across a net. Further practice for serving should include specific placement of serves: down sidelines both long and short; long and short cross court; long and short center court.

SPIKE

The spike is an offensive skill and the primary point winner in highly skilled games. Theoretically, each team attempts to receive the ball from the opposing team with a pass to a "setter" who then sets or passes the ball in such a way that it may be spiked into the opponent's court. This is not always

Fig. 8.6. Spike

possible, even in skillful play, but it is the basic pattern of the game. A successful spike attempt is greatly dependent upon a good set.

The potential spiker is usually at the left or right forward or front position. She is positioned near the sideline approximately eight feet from the net. The right-handed spiker on the left side of the net and the left-handed spiker on the right side of the net will position a few feet outside the sideline. In this position, the potential spiker is facing the net and watching the setter. As the setter contacts the ball, the spiker must time her approach and jump to the height and direction of the ball. Assuming a regular arcing set, the spiker usually begins her approach as, or just after, the setter contacts the ball. There are two methods of approaching the net in preparation for the spike. Both are used by skillful players, and each player can determine which is best for her. In one approach, the player moves forward, and from a one-foot takeoff, lands on two feet simultaneously with knees flexed ready for the upward thrust of the jump. In the other approach, the player takes two steps toward the net and brings the first foot alongside the second foot, and the knees flex in preparation for the jump. In both approaches, the player moves to build forward momentum that will be transferred to upward momentum in the jump. As the player moves toward the jump, the arms fall behind her body in preparation for the upward thrust. The player then thrusts upward with an extension of the knees and an upward swing of the arms. The striking arm is brought behind the line of the body with backward shoulder rotation. The elbow is bent and the wrist hyperextended. The player begins the forward swing of the striking movement just as she reaches the apex of her jump. The elbow leads and extends, and contact is made with the heel of the hand followed by the hand and fingers as a result of a quick flexion of the wrist. The follow-through of the arm is in the direction of the ball, and the spiker lands on both feet. *Rules differ on whether or not a player may follow through over the net on a spike.*

PROGRESSION AND TEACHING SUGGESTIONS

The most common errors in spiking are:

1. Failing to transfer forward momentum to upward momentum, carrying the player very close or into the net.
2. Stopping after the approach and before the jump, thereby losing momentum.
3. Mistiming or misjudging the approach and jump with the ball.
4. Striking the ball with a closed fist, hoping to achieve power but resulting in a loss of power and accuracy.

The most obvious problem with the spike is that some girls and women are too small or cannot jump high enough to spike effectively. While all beginners should attempt to spike, it will become apparent that some are almost incapable of spiking a ball downward into the opponent's court. At this point, the overhead set and the role of the setter in general should be stressed. Not only does the spike depend upon a good set, but it also gives an alternative role to those who have difficulty spiking. This is not to infer that players are divided at this point into spikers and setters. Often the small, unlikely appearing player will have a surprising ability in jumping and will become a successful spiker. However, after a reasonable amount of practice, many players will begin to discover their own limitations and abilities and seek the roles most appropriate for them. Because volleyball does not require that everyone *must* spike the ball, there is no reason why the totally unsuccessful spiker must continue to futilely attempt a spiking skill. Many of the best setters in the game have little ability in spiking.

Much attention should be paid to the approach and jump. The player must be able to position herself correctly according to the flight of the ball and must approach and jump almost instinctively before she can really be concerned and consistent with the hit of the ball.

DRILLS

1. Singly, in partners, or in small groups, each player holds the ball about shoulder height and hits the ball toward the ground. This is increased to a short toss into the air.
2. Singly, with partners, or in short lines, each player faces the wall about ten feet away, tosses the ball up, and hits it to the ground, causing it to rebound up off the wall. The player then attempts to spike the rebound, and the process is continuous.
3. All players spread out within an area and practice the approach. First on a count of *one* and *two—three*, then on their own.
4. In lines or along the left or right sideline, each player attempts her approach. Then to get the feel of the hit without the problem of timing with the set, one person standing on a chair holds the ball just above net level as player approaches and spikes the ball out of the supporting hand.
5. Players form lines along left or right sideline with one player in center for-

ward or front position. Center forward tosses a ball, simulating a set, for each player to spike. This basic drill then increases in difficulty to:

a. A set from the center forward rather than a toss.
b. Spiker passes the ball to center forward who sets for the spiker.
c. Player in center back position passes to center forward who sets for spiker.

Practice should be on both the left and right sides of the net for both left- and right-handed spikers. The setters should alternate, providing practice in setting as well as in spiking.

BLOCK

The block is a defense against a possible spike. Basically, the skill is just what its name implies. One or two players on the defensive team attempt to block the spiked ball so as to send the ball directly back into the opponent's court or deflect the spike and slow it down.

Blocking is basically a matter of positioning and timing a jump with the spiker's hit. A one-player block utilizes just one front-row player. In a two-player block a front-row player moves in next to another front-row player to give greater coverage on the block. The blocker, watching the ball and the spiker, is positioned approximately one foot away from the net.

The blocker's jump is timed just after the spiker begins her jump. This timing, of course, depends on the type of set. As the blocker jumps, facing the net, she extends both arms up and diagonally forward with firm open hands. The thumbs of the two hands are only a few inches apart and the

Fig. 8.7. Block

3. Hands too far apart, permitting a spike between them.
4. Second blocker jumps into first blocker on a two-player block.
5. Closing the eyes while blocking.

When possible, a two-player block is usually more effective than a one-player block. The second blocker must move quickly sideward and jump straight up so as not to jump into the first blocker. The second blocker may touch the first blocker with her hand to judge how close she is to her. The two closest hands of the two blockers should be only a few inches apart so that the ball cannot be spiked between them.

The most difficult aspect of a successful block is the timing of the jump. This becomes more difficult in advanced play, as the sets may intentionally vary greatly to confuse opponents.

wrists slightly hyperextended. *Rules may differ on whether or not the player or players may reach over the net to block.* A hard-hit spike will rebound off the blocker's hands. When allowed to reach over the net to block, the blocker or blockers attempt to place their hands over the ball to block. As the blocker returns to the ground, she must pull her hands back to avoid contact with the net.

PROGRESSION AND TEACHING SUGGESTIONS

The most common errors in blocking are:

1. Mistiming the jump, usually jumping too soon.
2. Jumping forward rather than straight up, resulting in a net foul.

DRILLS

1. Players face a partner across the net with as many players as necessary or possible on each side. On a count, both players, without a ball, jump as in a block. Players then can alternate in the roles of spiker and blocker, the blocker timing her jump to that of the spiker.

2. Players in twos, facing their partner across the net, begin at one end of the net. One player acts as a spiker, the other as a blocker. The spiker moves sidewards two steps and executes the movements of a spike. The blocker follows the spiker's movements and attempts a block, all without a ball. Players continue the width of the net.

3. Using a spiking drill, for example, spiking drill number 5, players rotate through the position of blocker for a

one-player block against each spiker. Later, another player is added for a two-player block attempt.

ONE-ARM FOREHAND PASS OR DIG

The one-arm underhand hit of the ball is used only when the player cannot possibly reach the ball with two arms. It is similar to the forearm pass, and it is useful in an emergency situation. It is a means of getting the ball into the air when it might otherwise drop to the floor if a two-handed stroke were attempted.

In every situation the player should attempt to get in a position for a two-handed hit. If this fails, as in a spike or deflection of the ball by a teammate, the player should reach for the ball with the closest arm, attempting to contact the ball with the forearm. In such an emergency hit, it is doubtful

that an accurate pass will result. The main objective is to keep the ball from hitting the floor and to get the ball into the air.

PROGRESSION AND TEACHING SUGGESTIONS

The most common errors in the one-hand forearm pass are:

1. Using a one-hand hit when it is possible to hit with two hands.
2. Swinging a fist in the direction of the ball rather than reaching with the forearm.

It cannot be emphasized too strongly that a one-hand hit is far inferior to a two-hand hit. Beginners may simply plant their feet and hit with one arm rather than move to a position for a two-hand hit after this skill has been introduced. Practice and play situations should emphasize the one-hand hit *only* when a two-hand hit is impossible.

Fig. 8.8. One-arm forehand pass or dig

Many of the drills indicated for practice of the forearm pass can be utilized for the one-hand forearm pass. In all cases, however, the player should attempt a two-hand hit when possible and use the one-hand hit only when necessary. Drills then will include practice of both hits, with the player differentiating between the use of each.

NET RECOVERY

The best net recovery is not allowing the ball to hit the net. This infers that a player should attempt an overhead or forearm hit before the ball hits the net, since a great percentage of net recoveries are unsuccessful. However, it is inevitable that occasionally the ball will be sent into the net. Players must be able to pass the ball to a teammate or send the ball over the net after it has contacted the net.

The player should stand with her side to the net. She must observe the velocity and trajectory of the ball and determine where the ball will hit the net and the force with which it will hit. If the ball hits high or low in the net, it will tend to fall vertically toward the floor, and the player must be positioned close to the net for recovery. If the ball hits the middle or belly of the net, it will tend to rebound back, and the player must position farther away from the net for recovery. The greater the force behind the ball, the greater the rebound. The ball will also tend to rebound at an equal but opposite angle from its approach, particularly when it hits in the middle of the net. Since a net recovery is very difficult to judge, the player should attempt to hit the ball with a forearm or one-arm forearm pass

Fig. 8.9. Net recovery

as close to the floor as possible. Allowing the ball to drop allows the time necessary for determination of the flight of the ball and allows the ball to rebound as far as possible away from the net. If the hit into the net is the second hit by the team, the player must attempt to put the ball over the net on the recovery hit. If the hit into the net is the first hit by the team, the player should attempt to get the ball into the air where a teammate can make a constructive and offensive hit into the opponent's court.

PROGRESSION AND TEACHING SUGGESTIONS

The most common errors in net recovery are:

1. Misjudging the flight and trajectory of the ball which can result in a miss, or hitting the ball back into the net or in an uncontrolled manner.
2. Standing too close to the net on a ball hitting the middle of the net, resulting in the ball flying past the player.
3. Standing too far away from the net on a ball hitting high or low on the net, resulting in a poorly hit ball usually traveling under the net.
4. Not making every attempt to hit the ball *before* it hits the net.

Successful net recoveries are low percentage hits. Players must experience and experiment with many different net recovery situations before they can become even somewhat competent. The concept of permitting the ball to fall close to the floor is contrary to natural instincts and is difficult for most beginners to accept. Practices should permit a wide variety of possible situations with some experimentation on the part of the players.

DRILLS

Drills for net recovery must take place at the net. Players should first attempt net recoveries as passes to a teammate and sending the ball over the net from a thrown ball. The trajectory and force of the ball should be varied. Later, the ball may be deliberately hit into the net for net recovery practice.

DINK

The dink is used as a change of pace when a spiker realizes that a block has been set against her. The object of a dink is to put the ball over or around the block. The dink should not be so high, wide, or deep as to permit the opponents to play the ball.

The player approaches the dink in the same manner as the spike. It is most important that the opponents do not realize that a dink is to be expected. Therefore, the dink is most effective when the player is in position to spike, not when she is off-balance or has mistimed her jump for the spike. As the spiker jumps, she reaches toward the ball with her fingers. She contacts the ball with the pads of her fingers, directing the ball just over the hands of the blocker or just to the sides of the blocker's hands. A dink over the hands of a blocker should land close behind the blocker to be effective. The dink may also be contacted with the heel of the hand or with a fist, but neither is as accurate as the fingertips.

PROGRESSION AND TEACHING SUGGESTIONS

The most common errors in dinking are:

1. Approaching slower and not jumping as high as in the spike.

Fig. 8.10. Dink

2. Popping the ball too high or too deep.
3. Allowing the ball to rest on the hand or pushing the ball, resulting in an illegal hit.

The dink can be very effective as a change of pace. On a suspected dink, blockers will back off the net, negating the block. The dink will cause the opponents to reposition, opening up the possibilities for the spike. However, the dink can be overused and become ineffective.

Practice for the dink is the same as practice for the spike, preferably with one or two blockers.

Selected Advanced Skills

The following skills may or may not be taught in the regular instructional program. They are the skills of the advanced player in competition. Emphasis in beginning and intermediate play should be on the basic skills of the game. Advanced skills are for those players who are competent in the basic skills. Teaching suggestions and drills are presented only when the skill is unlike those presented in the beginning and intermediate sections.

BACK SET

The back set allows the setter to pass the ball to the spiker directly behind her. Thus, without moving, the setter in the center forward or front position can set to either spiker. Part of the effectiveness of this hit is the deception. The opponents are not sure which spiker will receive the ball until the ball is hit. The back set is similar to the front set until the ball is contacted. On contact, the fingers point backward and the back is arched. The follow-through is back and up in the direction of the ball.

BACK FOREARM PASS

The back forearm pass is used when the player is caught out of position with her back to the intended flight of the ball and the ball is too low to pass overhead. Whenever she can, the player should attempt to face the direction of the pass; however, this is not always possible. The player is positioned as in the front forearm pass. The ball is contacted close to the body and above shoulder height. The upper body must lean backward to permit the hit to go up and over the head. For long passes, the arms may swing up to contact the ball.

PASS AND ROLL

When receiving a spike or reaching for a low, wide dig, the player may be off-balance after contacting the ball. In the situation where the player receives a hard-hit spike in a basically balanced position, she must absorb some of the force of the ball through her body; otherwise the ball may rebound too great a distance. In this case, the player contacts the ball low, shifting her weight back on contact. This will cause the player to roll backwards. If the momentum is not great, the player should recover forward to her feet as soon as possible. With greater momentum or when the player is reaching for the ball and is pulled off-balance, she may execute a roll over her shoulder, coming to her feet as soon as possible. This modified shoulder roll has been referred to as the Japanese roll. As the player reaches for the low ball, her knees are flexed and her body low. As she loses balance after contact with the ball, the player lands in a semi-seated position or slightly on one hip. She rolls diagonally across her back and over the opposite shoulder. One or both knees are tucked on the roll and assist in getting the player back to her feet quickly after the roll is completed.

It should be stressed that the pass and roll is executed only when necessary. Although when executed correctly, the roll gets the player back into play faster than if she simply sprawled on the floor from an off-balance hit, there is a period of time when the player is completely out of the play. Some players find the roll fascinating and use it at every opportunity, but they actually diminish their effectiveness as players.

Practice in the pass and roll should begin on a padded surface such as a mat. Rolling incorrectly on the floor can produce bruises on the body.

STRATEGY

Offense and defense can shift rapidly in volleyball. Basically, the team with the ball is potentially on the offense, while the team waiting to receive the ball is on defense. Since points can only be won by the serving team, this team is basically on the offense during the term of service. If a team is unable to produce a spike or well-directed hit to the opponent's court, they are said to be hitting defensively. Volleyball has no direct interaction of the two teams. The only exception is when a spiker and blocker contact the ball simultaneously over the net. Otherwise, the net separates the two teams.

Volleyball consists of a match in which the first team to win two games is the winner. A game consists of fifteen points or eight minutes of playing time, whichever occurs first. A team must lead by two points to win. Each team attempts to score as many points as possible as quickly as possible and to prevent their opponents from scoring. It is toward these respective ends that all strategy is aimed.

Basic strategy is presented as being basic to *all* levels of play.

Offensive Strategy

Ideally, *all* players on a team should be able to set and spike effectively; however, this rarely occurs. Offensive strategy begins with the determination of spikers and setters. In beginning play, where all players are experiencing the game and positions equally, it is easiest to designate the center forward or front position as the setter. This means that whichever player is in that position at the time acts as the setter. This is a modification of the most popular offensive system, the 4–2 system.

In the 4–2 or four-spiker, two-setter system, four players are the primary spikers and two are the primary setters, regardless of their initial position on the court. The setters are positioned with two spikers between them in the serving order. The first pass will always be directed toward the center forward position for the set to either of the two side spikers. When a setter is in the center forward position, this presents no problem. When a setter is in the left or right forward position, she must begin on that side of the net and switch to the center forward position on the serve of the ball. *The rules require that each player be in correct serving order on the serve, with each of the three forward line players ahead of their respective back line players. No part of one player's body may overlap with any part of another player's body.* On each rotation, one setter will be in a front-line position.

The 5–1 offense requires five spikers and one setter. The positioning is the same as in the 4–2 offense when the setter is in the front line. When the setter rotates to the back line, she waits behind her respective front-line player and moves to the net on the serve. In the 5–1 offense, three players are potential spikers when the setter is in the back row. This offense requires that the one setter be very quick and possess endurance.

The 6–0 offense utilizes all six players as possible spikers and setters. The setter is usually the player in the right back position, allowing three spikers at the net.

The 6–2 offense requires that all players be able to spike but only two act as setters. The back-row setter, as opposed to the front-row setter in the 4–2 offense, moves to the net on the serve, permitting three potential spikers at the net.

Although the team with the serve is employing an offensive technique, the positioning is defensive, ready to receive the opponent's return. Defensive positioning is also employed when the opposing team is serving. Both types of defensive positioning are discussed in the section on defensive strategy.

Once the ball is received from the opponents, the team is on the offense, if they can control the ball. The basic pattern of offense is to receive the ball from the opponents with a forearm pass to a setter who then sets for a spiker. The spiker directs the ball downward to an uncovered space in the opponent's court. Therefore, offense is not simply "getting the ball over the net somehow." The basic pattern assumes that the opponent's serve or return can be controlled by the first player to play the ball. This is the point where the offense breaks down most readily. When the first hit is not controlled, it is difficult for the second player to both control and set the ball for a spiker. In this case it becomes a matter of getting the ball in the air in a position where the third player can at least direct the ball deep into the opponent's court or to some uncovered space. The last resort of a team is to somehow get the ball over the net on the third hit, no matter where or how the player must play the ball.

The second point where the offense breaks down is on the set. The spiker must be aware that no matter how bad the set, she must send the ball over the net into the opponent's court. It is not constructive for the team if the spiker blames the loss of a point or serve on a poor set. This requires that the spiker approach the spike positively, yet be able to reposition in the event of a poor set that is too low, over her head, or too short.

The third point of breakdown is on the spike itself. Beginning spikers may become discouraged with their attempts when they result in the ball being hit out-of-bounds or into the net. In some cases, the spiker may cease to attempt the spike, preferring to "play it safe." At this point the greatest offensive skill is lost.

Whenever a player spikes, there is the possibility of a successful block, sending the ball directly back at the spiker. Since the spiker will usually be unable to play the ball, the other members of the team should cover the spiker to protect against the successful block. In general, the closest three players form a semicircle directly behind the spiker, the remaining two players in position to cover for a ball bouncing deep off a block.

GENERAL OFFENSIVE STRATEGY

1. The team must be able to switch quickly from offense to defense.

2. The type of offensive system used will depend upon the competencies of the players.
3. Left-handed spikers can be very confusing to a defense.
4. When switching positions after the serve, players should move quickly and decisively.

Defensive Strategy

Defensive strategy is basically positioning and attempting to block the spiker.

When the opposing team is serving, the basic defensive positioning is as shown in figure 8.11. This diagram shows a setter in the center front position ready for a 4–2, modified 4–2, or 5–1 offense. As indicated in the offensive strategy section, this basic positioning changes slightly when the setter is positioned in the left or right forward position for the 4–2 offense, or in the 5–1

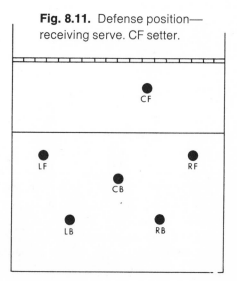

Fig. 8.11. Defense position—receiving serve. CF setter.

offense with the setter in the back row, or in the 6–0 or 6–2 offenses.

When the opposing team is attempting a spike, the positioning for the defensive team is one that permits a block of the spike.

When a team is receiving a spike, they position with three forwards in their respective positions at the net ready for a block. The center back is approximately ten feet behind the center forward, and the left and right

Fig. 8.12. Defense position— receiving serve. RF setter.

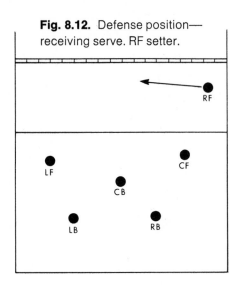

Fig. 8.14. Defensive positioning against spike

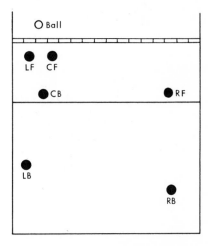

a. Basic defense position against spike.

Fig. 8.13. Defense position— receiving serve. Setter in back row.

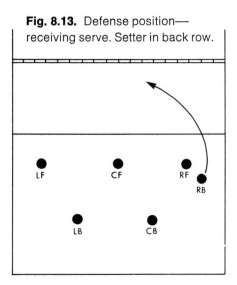

b. Blocking position against spike.

backs are toward the rear corners of the court. When the ball is set to an opposing spiker, the player directly opposite and the other closest forward will form a two-player block. The remaining forward drops back from the net to protect against the cross-court spike. The center back moves behind the blockers to protect against a dink or a rebound off the blockers. The remaining two backs move in, depending on the position of the spiker, one to protect against spikes down the sideline, the other against cross-court spikes.

The alternate defensive positioning places the center back deep in the court rather than ten feet behind the center forward. This defense places an additional player in the back court to cover long spikes but does not cover for the dink or rebound off the blockers.

If the opponents are not able to spike, the defensive team drops back into a position similar to that for receiving the serve.

GENERAL DEFENSIVE STRATEGY

1. The team must be able to move quickly from defense to offense and back again to defense.

2. If a blocker contacts the ball, she should call "one," indicating to her team that only two contacts remain.

3. Front-row players should allow serves higher than their waist to be played by back-row players.

4. Calling for a ball that is between two players is advisable to avoid collisions or a ball dropping to the floor.

BASIC UNIT PLAN FOR BEGINNERS

The following represents a guide for eighteen lessons in beginning volleyball. Specific warm-up and review are not included, as the instructor should select those most appropriate for her particular situation. It is suggested that warm-up be specifically related to the game. Practice stations refers to the division of the entire group into smaller groups for the simultaneous practice of different skills in different areas. These practice stations can include tasks of a skill test type to provide feedback and motivation for the learner. Although time is indicated in the unit plan for officiating, rules, and strategy, much of these areas are best covered as situations develop in play and in conjunction with skills presentations. It is suggested that some time during each lesson after lesson number 3 be devoted to play.

Lesson 1	Forearm pass—ready position
Lesson 2	Overhead pass
Lesson 3	Modified game
Lesson 4	Underhand serve—play
Lesson 5	Game—positioning—rules
Lesson 6	Overhead serve—play
Lesson 7	Game—officiating
Lesson 8	Spike and set
Lesson 9	Block—play
Lesson 10	Game—offensive and defensive strategy
Lesson 11	One-hand forearm pass—play
Lesson 12	Net recovery—dink
Lesson 13	Practice stations
Lesson 14	Game
Lesson 15–18	Tournament play

SELECTED BIBLIOGRAPHY

DGWS. *Volleyball Guide.* Washington, D.C.: AAHPER. Published every two years.

EGSTROM, GLEN H., and SCHAAFSMA, FRANCES. *Volleyball.* 2nd ed. Dubuque, Ia.: Wm. C. Brown Co. Publishers, 1972.

KELLER, VAL. *Point, Game and Match.* Hollywood: Creative Sports Books, 1968.

SCATES, ALLEN E., and WARD, JANE. *Volleyball.* Boston: Allyn & Bacon, Inc., 1969.

SCHAAFSMA, FRANCES, and HECK, ANN. *Volleyball for Coaches and Teachers.* Dubuque, Ia.: Wm. C. Brown Co. Publishers, 1971.

THIGPEN, JANET. *Power Volleyball for Girls and Women.* 2nd ed. Dubuque, Ia.: Wm. C. Brown Co. Publishers, 1973.

Glossary

Basketball

BACK COURT. That half of the court containing the opponent's basket.

BLOCKING. A foul involving body contact that impedes the progress of an opponent.

CHARGING. A foul in which the player with the ball moves to make contact with an opponent.

CLOSELY GUARDED. Guarding within three feet of the player with the ball.

DEAD BALL. A ball which is temporarily out of play.

DEFENSIVE PLAYER. A player whose team does not have the ball.

DRIBBLE. A skill in which the player gives impetus to the ball one or more times, causing it to rebound from the floor.

FAST BREAK. A maneuver to move the ball quickly down the court so as to have more offensive than defensive players.

FEINT. A deceptive movement to distract an opponent.

FREE THROW. An unguarded shot for goal after a foul has been called.

FRONT COURT. That half of the court containing a team's own basket.

JUMP BALL. Putting the ball in play by tossing it up between two opponents.

KEY. That part of the free throw lane between the free throw line and the end line.

LAY-UP SHOT. A shot close to the basket executed from a pass or dribble.

OFFENSIVE PLAYER. A player whose team has possession of the ball.

PICK. A type of screen that allows an offensive player with the ball to move past a defensive player. Also called screen and roll or pick and roll.

PIVOT. A move in which the player with the ball steps one or more times in any direction with the same foot while maintaining contact with the floor with the other foot.

PLAYER-TO-PLAYER DEFENSE. Each defensive player is assigned a specific offensive player to guard.

POST PLAYER. A player on the offensive team positioned in or near the key.

REBOUND. Gaining possession of a ball, shot at the basket, that has not scored.

SCREEN. The setting of a stationary block on a defensive player in order to prohibit her from guarding the player with the ball.

SET SHOT. A shot for basket taken from a stationary position with one or two hands.

TIE BALL. When two players of opposing teams place one or both hands firmly on the ball at the same time or a player places one or both hands firmly on a ball held by an opponent.

TIP-IN. A means of returning the ball toward the basket as a shot from a rebound without returning to the floor between the rebound and the subsequent shot.

TRAVELING. Illegal progression in any direction while in possession of the ball in bounds.

TWO-STEP STOP. One method of completing a catch or dribble while on the run so as not to travel.

VIOLATION. An infringement of the rules for which the ball is put in play from out-of-bounds by the opposing team.

ZONE DEFENSE. Defensive players cover the player with the ball and primary spaces rather than actively guarding all offensive players.

Field Hockey

ADVANCING. A foul committed when a player contacts the ball with a part of her body and gains an advantage.

ATTACK. Those players designated as forward line players.

BULLY. A means of starting each half, after each goal, and used in the case of a double foul or injury.

CORNER. Awarded to the attacking team when the defending team has caused the ball to go out-of-bounds over their end line.

COVERING. A defensive strategy in which one or more players are not marking players but are covering spaces to protect against the possibility of an attacking player losing her opponent and against long passes.

DANGEROUS HIT. A foul committed when a player has undercut the ball, hit directly into an opponent, or played the ball in such a way as to cause it to rise dangerously.

DEFENSE. Those players designated as or playing the position of halfback, fullback, or goalkeeper.

DEFENSIVE TEAM. The team not in possession of the ball.

DODGE. A means of evading a potential tackler while maintaining possession of the ball.

DRIBBLE. A means of advancing the ball on the ground with a series of short taps.

DRIVE. A means of hitting the ball moderate to long distances.

FIELDING. Gaining possession of the ball from a pass or interception.

FLICK. A means of putting the ball into the air over moderate to long distances.

FREE HIT. Awarded to the opposing team after a breach of the rules or out-of-bounds except for corner, penalty corner, roll-in, or penalty bully situations.

JAB. An emergency spoiling stroke used when a tackle is not possible.

MARKING. A defensive strategy in which the defensive player is between her opponent and goal, within a stick's length, and positioned for an interception of any pass directed toward her opponent.

OBSTRUCTION. A foul committed by running between an opponent and the ball, interposing the body or stick as an obstruction.

OFFENSIVE TEAM. The team in possession of the ball.

OFFSIDE. A foul by the offensive team when they gain advantage by having a player or players ahead of the ball in the opponent's end of the field when it is hit or rolled with less than three opponents between the player or players and the goal line.

PENALTY BULLY. Awarded when a sure goal has been stopped by a breach of the rules or in the case of a willful or repeated foul committed by the defense in the striking circle.

PENALTY CORNER. Awarded when the defending team commits a foul in the striking circle or intentionally sends the ball over the end line.

QUICK HIT. Hitting the ball with the same grip as in the dribble.

REVERSE STICK. Turning the stick over in order to play the ball on the left side of the body.

ROLL-IN. Awarded to an opponent of the

player who causes the ball to go out-of-bounds over a sideline.

SCOOP. A means of putting the ball into the air over short distances.

STICKS. A foul committed when a player raises any part of her stick above her shoulder when involved in the play of the ball.

STRIKING CIRCLE. The area and lines in front of each goal, marked by a line four yards long, parallel to, and sixteen yards from the goal and continued to meet the goal line by quarter circles.

TACKLE. A means of taking the ball away from an opponent.

Lacrosse

BODY CHECKING. A means of slowing down a player with the ball by a defensive player placing her body between the opponent with the ball and the direction she is attempting to run, without actual body contact.

CRADLING. A basic skill of the game used to keep the ball in a player's stick.

CREASE. The 8½-foot radius circle surrounding each goal cage.

CROSSE CHECK. An attempt to dislodge the ball from an opponent's stick with a controlled tap or series of taps with the stick.

CUTTING. Movements of the offensive team to get free of their opponents in anticipation of a pass.

DEFENSE. Those players designated as or playing the position of center, defense wing, third man, cover point, point, or goalkeeper.

DEFENSE INTERCHANGE. Defensive system in which a free attack player may be covered or checked.

DEFENSIVE TEAM. The team not in possession of the ball.

DODGE. A means of evading an opponent while maintaining possession of the ball.

DRAW. Method of starting play at the beginning of each half and after each goal.

FREE POSITION. Awarded to the opponents after a foul or an infringement of the rules.

MARKING. Defensive strategy in which each defense player is between her opponent and goal and within one or two feet in position for an interception should a pass be directed toward her opponent.

OFFENSE. Those players designated or playing the position of center, attack wing, or home.

OFFENSIVE TEAM. The team in possession of the ball.

STAND. When an umpire blows her whistle, the ball is dead, and all players must stand where they are at the time of the whistle.

THROW. The throw is awarded to two opposing players in the case of two players being equally near a ball out-of-bounds, a double foul, an injury not involving a foul, or a ball lodging in the crosse or body of a player, except the goalkeeper.

Soccer, Speedball, Speed-a-way

BLOCK. A means of controlling the ball when it is in the air.

CORNER KICK. Awarded to the opponents when the defending team has caused the ball to go out-of-bounds over their end line.

COVERING. A defensive strategy in which one or more players cover spaces rather than marking specific players.

DEFENSE. Those players designated or playing the position of halfback, fullback, or goalkeeper.

DEFENSE KICK. Awarded to the defending team when the attacking team causes the ball to go out-of-bounds over the end line.

DEFENSIVE TEAM. The team not in possession of the ball.

DIRECT FREE KICK. A free kick from which a goal may be scored directly.

DODGE. A means of evading an opponent while maintaining possession of the ball.

DRIBBLE. A means of advancing the ball on the ground with a series of taps with the feet.

DROPKICK. A means of kicking the ball with a low, hard trajectory, over moderate distances, contacting the ball just after it hits the ground.

HEADING. Volleying the ball with the head.

INDIRECT FREE KICK. A free kick from which a goal may not be scored directly.

LIFT. Method of converting a ground ball to an aerial ball.

MARKING. A defensive strategy in which a player defends against a specific opponent.

OFFENSE. Those players designated or playing the position of forward.

OFFENSIVE TEAM. The team in possession of the ball.

OFFSIDE. A foul when a team gains advantage by having a player or players ahead of the ball in the opponent's end of the field when it is kicked or thrown with less than three opponents between the player or players and the end line.

PENALTY KICK. Awarded for fouls committed by a player of the defending team within the penalty area.

PLACE KICK. Kicking a stationary ball.

PUNT. A means of kicking the ball in the air

over long distances, contacting the ball with the foot before it hits the ground.

RESTRAINING LINE. Drawn from sideline to sideline, five yards from and on each side of the halfway line.

TACKLE. A means of securing possession of the ball from an opponent.

THROW-IN. A means of putting the ball in play after it has gone out-of-bounds over a sideline.

TRAP. A means of controlling a ball on the ground.

VOLLEY. Rebounding the ball off the body as a pass to a teammate.

Softball

BACKING UP. One fielder moving behind another to cover in case of an error.

BASE ON BALLS. A batter receiving four balls before three strikes and advancing to first base. A walk.

BATTERY. The pitcher and catcher as a unit.

BATTING ORDER. Sequence in which the offensive team comes to bat.

BUNT. A short surprise hit used to advance a base runner or as an infield base hit.

DEFENSIVE TEAM. The team in the field.

DOUBLE. A two-base hit.

DOUBLE PLAY. Two outs are made on the offensive team in one play.

ERROR. A misplayed ball that is judged avoidable.

FIELDER'S CHOICE. A play in which a fielder can choose which runner to attempt to put out.

HIT AND RUN. An offensive play in which the batter will hit the next pitch and the base runner is off to the next base on the pitch.

INNING. When both teams have committed three outs as the offensive team.

OFFENSIVE TEAM. The team at bat.

PLACE HITTING. Hitting the ball to a specific spot on the field.

RELAY THROW. Used when an outfielder cannot reach the infield with a direct throw.

SACRIFICE. A hit in which the primary objective is to advance a runner already on base.

SLIDE. Lowering the body to a horizontal position in order to avoid being tagged out when advancing from one base to another.

SQUEEZE PLAY. A player attempting to steal from third base to home.

STOLEN BASE. Advancing from one base to another without the benefit of a hit or walk.

TRIPLE. A three-base hit.

Volleyball

BACK SET. An overhead pass directed behind the player passing the ball.

BLOCK. A defensive maneuver against a spike in which one or more defensive players attempt to stop the spike as it crosses the net.

BUMP. Also called forearm pass.

DEFENSIVE TEAM. The team receiving the serve or waiting to receive the ball from the opposing team.

DIG. Also called one-arm forearm pass. Similar to forearm pass except the player can only reach the ball with one arm.

DINK. A deceptive short hit over the blockers.

FLOATER SERVE. An overhand serve in which there is no spin on the ball and it appears to float in the air.

FOOT FAULT. Server steps on or over the end line at the moment she contacts the ball.

FOREARM PASS. Also called the forearm bump, dig, or bounce pass. Skill in which the ball rebounds off both forearms.

ILLEGAL HIT. Ball visibly comes to rest momentarily on any part of the body.

NET RECOVERY. Playing the ball after it hits the net before three hits have been taken by a team.

OFFENSIVE TEAM. The serving team or the team in control of the ball.

READY POSITION. Basic position to receive the ball.

SET. An overhead pass in which the ball is hit in a controlled manner for the spiker to hit.

SERVE. An underhand or overhand hit used to put the ball in play.

SPIKE. An offensive hit directed to a space in the opponent's court with a downward motion.

Index